Dundee

THE CITY GUIDE

DUNDEE

ONE CITY, MANY DISCOVERIES

Edited by Catharina Day
& Sarah Milne

Catharina Day is a writer of three guide books including *The Cadogan Guide to Ireland*. She has lived with her family near Dundee for over 20 years

Contributors: Niki Boyle, William Calder, Hannah Ewan, Caroline Gibb, Anna Millar, Tom Sampson
With thanks to the contributors from the 2010 edition of the Dundee City Guide

Design: Gavin Munro

Images courtesy of:

Front Cover: Nicole Guarino, Scottish Dance Theatre
Ken Bushe
micheledillon.co.uk
Dundee City Council
James Howie: © The Artist's estate
© Royal Commission on the Ancient and Historical Monuments of Scotland;
D/36106/cn.
Licensor www.scran.ac.uk
Scottish Viewpoint
The University of Dundee
V & A at Dundee
VisitScotland
And individual venues listed

© 2012 The List Ltd
ISBN: 978-0-9557513-5-6

Extensive efforts have been made to ensure the accuracy of the information in this publication, however the publishers can accept no responsibilty for any errors it may contain.

Published by The List Ltd
14 High Street
Edinburgh EH1 1TE
Tel: 0131 550 3050

Printed and bound by
Scotprint, Haddington

Contents

V&A AT DUNDEE
MAKING IT HAPPEN

V&A at Dundee will be an international centre for design, housed in a world-class building at the heart of Dundee's waterfront.

It will host major exhibitions, celebrate our design heritage, inspire and promote contemporary talent, and encourage design innovation for the future.

V&A at Dundee will become a centre for everyone – a place to enjoy and be proud of.

Get involved with the project online and sign up for regular updates:

www.VandAatDundee.com

Welcome to Dundee

Since the first edition of the Dundee City Guide was published, the city has already changed so much.

One of the most exciting projects leading the transformation of the city is at the Waterfront, which over the next few years, will be turned into a welcoming green space filled with shops, cafés, offices and public art – reconnecting the city to the water.

Leading the way is the V&A at Dundee, which will play a vital role in the city's ambitious plans for regeneration. Work on the iconic building is planned to start in 2013, with an opening date sometime in 2015. Before the new building opens, the city will play host to some of the V&A exhibitions, so we won't have to wait too long before its influence is felt in Dundee.

Dundee's new lease of life is also attracting other famous names to invest in the city – the hotel chain Malmaison have leased the old Tay Hotel building, a landmark for anyone arriving by train, and are now in the process of refurbishing it, with a 91 bedroom hotel set to open in spring 2013. Bold new plans for the train station itself will mean that visitors to Dundee get a great welcome to the city.

Café culture has sprung up, with lots of independent cafés opening all over – great places to catch up with friends over a cup of tea and some delicious homemade cakes.

And studying in Dundee has never been more attractive – Dundee University was recently rated as the best in the UK for student experience by The Times Higher Education Survey, while Ignite, the city's 10-day cultural festival, showcases the Degree Show at Duncan of Jordanstone College of Art & Design.

This unique guide will give you a taster of all the exciting things happening in the city, and I hope that when you visit Dundee you'll fall in love with all it has to offer. **lorrainekelly.tv**

How to use

Within each category, entries are arranged alphabetically and contain the following information

Address & telephone number
■ All entries are located within Dundee, unless otherwise indicated.

Opening hours
■ Opening hours are correct at time of going to press. For a restaurant or café, a distinction is made between opening hours and food served hours, if applicable.

Description
■ A general description of the establishment, attraction or activity, with relevant information on its style, atmosphere, clientele, facilities and services offered.

Westport Gallery
■ 48 Westport, 01382 221751; Mon–Sat 9am–5pm. Closed Sun

A sophisticated Aladdin's cave, Westport Gallery sells an array of arty pieces. Known and named for its artwork, a variety of prints and pictures are available at the gallery including amazing digital shots and paintings of the bridges over the Tay and other Dundee landmarks. **wpgal.co.uk**

Website for the area, venue or business
■ Where possible a website is provided (minus the www.), where more information should be available.

Want to discover more about Dundee?

visit dundee.com

- Check out What's On

- Meet local people on our Dundee and Me section

- Find out more about what Dundonians think of their city

- Learn about our innovators and ambassadors

- Get further details of what to do here and where to stay

- Read the latest news from the city

It's all on dundee.com

DUNDEE
ONE CITY, MANY DISCOVERIES

Attractions 12-23

Culture 24-39

Activities 40-51

Shop 52-63

Dundee's bright future

The ancient city of Dundee is situated in a beautiful and fortunate position – where the River Tay meets the North Sea. Over the years it has seen both good and bad fortune, but it could be argued that Dundee is on the verge of entering its prime with a forward looking master plan which will revitalise the expansive waterfront area of the city, and in turn generate redevelopment and investment in other areas.

As an important settlement since the 12th century, Dundee has certainly had some ups and downs, but since 2000 things have definitely been looking up for the city as it has reinvented itself as one City with many Discoveries – with much more to offer than Scott's famous ship, though this is still a definite must-visit for any visitor or local. Dundee's scientific prowess is once again leading the world, with important research being carried out at its two universities, and a games industry which continues to generate a thriving, modern economy for the city.

THE SUCCESS OF NEW INDUSTRIES ADDS TO THE BUZZ

The success of these new industries coupled with the Waterfront redevelopment all add to the buzz around Dundee at the present time.

Integral to the Waterfront plan is of course, the V&A at Dundee, a centre for design, beside Scott's Discovery. At one time, Dundee was known all over the world for its whaling and linen industries as well as the manufacture of jute. Jam and journalism also became important to Dundee's

prosperity, and DC Thomson is still an important employer here publishing the *The Courier* and *Beano*. The decline of traditional industries hit the city hard but recently biomedical, biochemical and biotechnical companies have joined the computer games industry in giving Dundee a modern economy. The redevelopment of the waterfront is central to Dundee's regeneration, and will take 30 years to complete. The port of Dundee will be a key site for offshore wind manufacturing and maintenance, and the city is committed to environmentally friendly development. New hotels, eating places and a refurbishment of the train station are planned and there is a wealth of cultural, educational and sporting resources waiting to be experienced by visitors, students and Dundonians alike.

Attractions

Whether you're looking for an exciting family day out or want to learn more about the history of the city, Dundee has plenty of attractions to suit everyone. Celebrate Dundee's maritime heritage, the arrival of jute and the new scientific excellence found in this inspiring city.

DUNDEE
ONE CITY, MANY DISCOVERIES

We've got it covered

Broughty Castle Museum
■ Castle Approach, Broughty Ferry, 01382 436916. Mon-Sat 10am-4pm; Sun 12.30-4pm. Oct-Mar: closed Mon
dundeecity.gov.uk/broughtycastle

See Culture, page 33.

Claypotts Castle
■ Broughty Ferry, outside access available at all times

Claypotts Castle is a terrific example of a 16th century Scottish z-plan towerhouse. With square rooms astride its towers as well as the original roof, Claypotts was once owned by John Graham of Claverhouse, 'Bonnie Dundee', who was killed at the Battle of Killiecrankie in 1689. Located in the middle of a housing estate off the main A92 Arbroath Road, just east of Dundee. **historic-scotland.gov.uk**

Claypotts Castle Z-plan towerhouse

Stephen Fry
Former rector of the University of Dundee, Stephen was awarded an honorary Doctor of Laws in 1995. Such is the university's affection for him, the main bar in the Students' Association building is named after his book, *The Liar*.

'Dundee's setting is probably more extraordinary than any other city in Scotland or Britain. It is about as ideal - ludicrously ideal - as any city setting can be.'

On the waterfront

Dundee's waterfront is one of the city's greatest attractions as the mighty Tay sweeps past it into the sea. There is a bold plan in the process of being executed to reconnect the waterfront with the city centre by rebuilding the city infrastructure, and although this will not be complete until 2021, massive improvements are taking place all the time.

Dundee's previous evolution may have somewhat cut off the centre from its waterfront; but this is quickly being reversed, as the Waterfront development aims to reconnect the city back to the river that once provided its lifeblood. Planners are making full use of the river, by encouraging more people to use it on a daily basis – and it's an area of the city that's constantly changing, so there's always something new to see. The grand plan includes pedestrian only areas, parks, restaurants, and bars. In particular, the new Kengo Kuma designed V&A building with its many social spaces will project into the Tay and take its place beside RRS Discovery by 2015.

THE WATER-FRONT TAKES IN GREEN WILDLIFE CORRIDORS, CYCLING, WALKING PATHS AND BEACHES

As part of the grand plan, some older buildings will be revamped. The railway station frontage is also to have a facelift and the Victorian Tay hotel, a landmark for any visitor to the city arriving by train is to be re-invented by the Malmaison hotel group. The waterfront extends along the Tay coastline from Grassy Beach in Broughty Ferry to Invergowrie Bay, taking in green wildlife corridors, cycling, walking paths and beaches, as well as the airport and the Port of Dundee.

The deep water port has just been designated as a new enterprise zone where great plans are afoot to concentrate on the renewable energy sector, especially the manufacture of offshore wind turbines. The Seabraes area of the waterfront is being promoted to attract digital media, and other sites will become available once the infrastructure rearrangement is complete.

The Waterfront redevelopment is all part of a £1 billion initiative, and so far about one third of the investment needed has been committed, so it is hoped that the new V&A at Dundee, with its emphasis on design will secure the further investment to make this huge transformation and build tourism in Dundee to a new level. **dundeewaterfront.com**

Dundee waterfront
The banks of the River Tay are undergoing a huge transformation, making this area central to the future vision of the city

RRS Discovery Captain Robert Scott's ship is a must-visit

RRS Discovery

■ Discovery Point, Discovery Quay, 01382 309060. Apr-Oct: Mon-Sat 10am-6pm; Sun 11am-6pm; Nov-Mar: 10am-5pm; Sun 11am-5pm. Closed Dec 25/26 & Jan 1/2; Admission: adults £8.25, conc £6.50, child £5, family £24 (discounted joint ticket with Verdant Works available)

As a major whaling centre, Dundee's shipyards had vast experience of constructing ships robust enough to travel through the Arctic pack ice. This expertise was put to use building RRS Discovery, the ship that was to be used for Captain Robert Scott's scientific exploration of Antarctica which began in 1901.

Nowadays, the RRS Discovery is one of Dundee's biggest attractions. Docked at the city's waterfront, it makes an impressive centrepiece to the city's ongoing regeneration. Visitors can explore the ship and find out what life on board was like. There are films and displays of scientific discoveries and artefacts to help bring to life the realities of that first expedition. Admire the three wooden masts on deck – it was the last ship of this type to be built in Britain – and try to imagine living in the cramped conditions below deck. Three meals a day were produced in the tiny galley and the Mess Deck was where all the men lived and slept (the officers were afforded some privacy in the spacious Wardroom deck).

It's a fascinating tale of one of the most heroic voyages of exploration ever undertaken, and makes for a fantastic family day out.
rrsdiscovery.com

Dundee Central Library
■ The Wellgate, 01382 431500. Mon/Tue & Thu/Fri 9am–6pm, Wed 10am–6pm, Sat 9.30am–5pm

Dundee Central Library is an oasis for family records and local history (including a collection of William McGonagall works). Check out the free monthly concerts in the Wighton room featuring works from the library's own collection of early Scottish music. This is the place to find out what is going on in the city: many venues in Dundee host classical ensemble concerts on a sporadic basis. Dundee Central Library is the busiest public library in Scotland and Dundee City Council's most visited public building. **dundeecity. gov.uk/library/central**

Mills Observatory
■ Glamis Road, Balgay Park, 01382 435967. **dundeecity. gov.uk/mills**

See Activities, page 50

HM Frigate Unicorn
■ Victoria Dock, 01382 200900. Apr-Oct: Mon–Sun 10am-5pm; Nov–Mar: Wed–Fri noon-4pm; Sat–Sun 10am-4pm. Closed Mon/Tue.

Last admission 30 minutes before closing. Admission £5.25; concession £4.25; child under 14 £3.25; family (2 adult 2 children) £13.75, (1 adult 2 children) £10.75, group (10 or more) £3.25/head

Billed as the world's oldest floating wooden warship, this wooden frigate is an anomaly in a world of shiny buildings, its ornate unicorn figurehead rearing up majestic and proud. Built in 1824, the ship was saved from a watery burial by a few enthusiasts, now known as the Unicorn Preservation Society. It is incredible to walk the decks of a warship built for sailing and to see the tough and cramped conditions within. The 18-pounder guns and the paraphernalia of the sailors littered among the modern notices add to the authenticity, as does the cold if you visit in winter. She survived because the Napoleonic wars finished and she was no longer needed for battle. Instead the hull was built over and training became her purpose.
frigateunicorn.org

Dundee Science Centre - Sensation
■ Greenmarket, 01382 228800. Mon–Sun 10am–5pm. Last admission 4pm. Admission £7.25; assisted needs adult £6.25; child (4–15) £5.25; special needs child £4.25; OAP/student £5.25; under 4s free. Holiday and annual passes available

Explore the science of the five senses through interactive shows and exhibits in this bright ten-year-old space. It

Jason Swedlow
Scientist, University of Dundee

'Dundee is a wonderful, safe and terrific place to raise a family and to grow personally and professionally. The city is a great place to start and develop a scientific career where innovation and new ideas are encouraged, supported and are all around you. The scientific environment is exciting, world leading and certainly part of the vibrancy that draws so many people here and ultimately keeps them here.'

DSC - Sensation Science family fun

is close to the railway station, shopping and the DCA and there's ample parking nearby – all pointing to a great place for a family day out. DSC - Sensation appeals to both children and adults, its exhibitions covering a wide spectrum of science presented in an exciting fashion. Interactivity is the order of the day, with plenty of red buttons for little hands to press and games to get involved in. Serious science is covered in an engaging way and there are temporary exhibitions and talks throughout the year.

The modern Infusion Coffee Shop sells light meals and hosts free discussions led by scientists from Dundee University every second Wednesday of the month at 6pm. This is just one of the ways the university reaches out to Dundonians.
sensation.org.uk

The Tay Bridges

Many people who have never even visited Dundee will still have heard of the Tay Rail Bridge disaster. The bridge linked Dundee and Fife, but collapsed in gale-force winds as a train was crossing it on 28 December, 1879. Everyone on board was lost in the cold waters of the Tay. The new bridge, opened in 1887, is still in use today and was designed to withstand future gales. Fourteen workers died during its construction. William McGonagall in a poem to the second Tay Bridge wrote, in his inimitable way: 'And your thirteen central girders which seem

Dundee's Maritime past and present

Dundee's location on a major estuary meant the development of a strong maritime industry. The manufacturing of jute created huge demand for whale oil in the 1900s, and the city soon became the premier British whaling port. Shipbuilding boomed, with over 2,000 ships built in the city over a ten year period.

But despite surviving the depression and seeing a rise in demand during World War II, the shipbuilding industry waned over the 20th century. Dundee saw the closure of five berths in 1981, with its shipbuilding coming to an end altogether in 1987.

After a dormant few years, the whole of the city's waterfront is now undergoing a 30 year, £1bn regeneration. Work is well underway, with the jewel in its crown – the V&A at Dundee – scheduled to open in 2015. The Victoria Docks have already been revitalised with retail and leisure development at City Quay. It is easy to revisit the past too – RRS Discovery, the ship taken to the Antarctic by Captain Scott, was built in Dundee in 1901. It returned to the city in 1986 and is moored next to a purpose-built visitors' centre.

■ rrsdiscovery.com
■ photopolis.dundeecity.gov.uk
■ dundeewaterfront.com

Trading up

One of the city's oldest civic groups, The Nine Incorporated Trades of Dundee, have moved into the 21st century with a website that tells the tale of the nine crafts that have contributed to trade growth over hundreds of years.

This growing repository of documents and imagery covers the history and customs associated with the traditional trades of Dundee: Bakers, Cordiners, Glovers, Tailors, Bonnetmakers, Butchers, Hammermen, Weavers and Dyers.

Their history dates back to 1124, when laws were passed for the regulation of various trades, and these regulations laid down standards to control price and quality.

From 1306, the trades were recognised as separate corporate bodies. But it soon became clear that they needed to act as a single body, and so The Nine Incorporated Trades of Dundee was set up, as early as 1581.

The group sees the future stretching ahead of them with the same sense of purpose that has been with them for over 800 years. In the words of their Honorary Archivist: 'Tradition for its own sake is worthless without a vision and a purpose for the future'.

■ **ninetradesofdundee.co.uk**

to my eye/Strong enough all windy storms to defy.'

That bridge gives wonderful views. The road bridge is less splendid but very practical, bringing the motorist straight into Dundee city centre. Road planning teams in the 1950s and 1960s created this traffic flow and in the process were accused of turning the city centre into a concrete wilderness. This has now been addressed through a ramp realignment programme.

Scotland's Jute Museum @ Verdant Works

■ West Henderson's Wynd, 01382 309060. Apr–Oct: Mon–Sat 10am–6pm; Sun 11am–6pm; Nov–Mar: Wed–Sat 10.30am-4.30pm; Sun 11am–4.30pm. Closed Mon/ Tue. Closed Dec 25/26 & Jan 1/2. Last admission one hour before closing. Admission £8.25; concession £6.50; child £5, family (2 adults, 2 children) £24. Discounted joint ticket available with Discovery Point

Set in the heartland of Dundee's jute factories, this attraction describes the jute industry and the impact it had on the city, where the hard life of the mills has left a permanent stamp. Before jute's prominence in 19th century Dundee, weaving had long brought in new blood, especially from Ulster. With jute, imported from India, Dundee grew massively. Women and children made up the bulk of the employees because they could be paid less. The displays and films illuminate the history of 19th and 20th century Dundee, its links with India and the lengthy process of making jute. There is also a permanent exhibition on the much-loved Broons.

THE TAY RAIL BRIDGE OPENED IN 1887 IS STILL IN USE TODAY

The Tay Bridge The Tay Rail Bridge is an iconic structure

Culture

Dundee is a city that's rich in culture, both historical and contemporary. From the beautifully refurbished McManus to the theatrical traditions of the Rep, this is a city that punches way above its weight in the arts. Exhibitions, contemporary dance and public art all help enrich the cultural landscape.

DUNDEE
ONE CITY, MANY DISCOVERIES

Art

Bonar Hall
■ Park Place, 01382 345466

A gift from a generous benefactor to the people of the city and University of Dundee, Bonar Hall is a vibrant venue. At the time of going to press, the University of Dundee were in talks with Dundee Rep to take over the lease of the venue in autumn 2012.
bonarhall.co.uk

Duncan of Jordanstone College of Art & Design
■ 13 Perth Rd, 01382 385330. Open during college hours

The college has a formidable reputation as one of the UK's best art schools and there is a constant stream of cutting edge exhibitions on offer at various locations throughout the campus and beyond – the Cooper Gallery, the Lower Foyer, the Bradshaw Gallery, the Matthew Gallery and Centrespace at the DCA. Each has a different emphasis and showcases work by students, teachers and international guests.

Themes for the exhibitions often link in with other disciplines taught in the university and the aim is to get students aware of how best to show their work. An ideal time to visit is the graduate show at the end of the summer semester.
exhibitions.dundee.ac.uk

Duncan of Jordanstone College of Art & Design Creative hub

Education, education, education

Famously a campus city, Dundee has a reputation for the highest standards in education. There is a strong link between academia and business, with the city considered a world leader in life sciences as well as in the creative industries.

■ University of Abertay Dundee

Top-rated in Scotland for environmental science research, with leading-edge initiatives such as the Abertay Centre for the Environment promoting 'green' business practices; the Urban Water Technology Centre; and the SIMBIOS unit exploring bioinformatics. Abertay also offers world-leading courses in Computer Arts and Computer Games Technology.
abertay.ac.uk

■ University of Dundee

In 2012 the University of Dundee was rated as the best in the UK for student experience by The Times Higher Education Survey, and in 2010, it was placed in the world's top 200 in the Times Higher Education Rankings. Its four main colleges – Art & Design, Architecture, Engineering and Physical Sciences; Arts and Social Sciences; Life Sciences; and Medicine, Dentistry and Nursing – are home to over 17,000 students, and it is seen as a centre for excellence by many industries across the world. The University is the first approved Cancer Research UK Centre in Scotland. **dundee.ac.uk**

■ Dundee College

This further education and higher education college is the only college in Dundee, the largest in Tayside and the 6th largest in Scotland. It attracts approximately 23,000 students each year. **dundeecollege.ac.uk**

■ Al-Maktoum College of Higher Education

A unique, independent, research-led centre of higher education for the study of Islam and Muslims. **almi.abdn.ac.uk**

V&A at Dundee

This exciting development, with an ambition to open in 2015, will create an international centre of design for Scotland. It is being developed by a partnership including the V&A in London, Dundee City Council, Scottish Enterprise and Dundee and Abertay Universities. The centre aims to be a source of inspiration and research for design in Scotland and hopes to foster the growth of its creative industries in which Dundee is already strong. It will also host international touring exhibitions from the V&A in London amongst other institutions.

The architectural design, by the Japanese practice Kengo Kuma and Associates, was chosen from over 120 entries after a fierce competition entered by national and international architects. The public were encouraged to view the plans of the six shortlisted practices on show in Dundee and to vote for their favourite before the choice was made – with over 15,000 visitors to the exhibition and many more online.

V&A at Dundee aims to create an outstanding building with unrivalled space for showing the best of design – from the past, present and the future. The building will extend out into the Tay close to RRS Discovery, its shape echoing that of its

Philip Long
Director, V&A at Dundee

'V&A at Dundee will contribute to the plans for growth of the city's prosperity and symbolise its renewed confidence and identity. The building, and the quality, scope and ambition of V&A at Dundee's exhibitions and programme will attract visitors locally, nationally and internationally. Building on the region's thriving creative sector, V&A at Dundee is helping shape the transformation of Dundee into one of Scotland - if not the UK's - most exciting cities.'

intrepid ocean-going neighbour, with a nod to the cliffs that form the barriers between the sea and land of the north east coast.

The eye-catching building, will itself be a star attraction adding to the appeal of the city and its waterfront area. It will house one of the largest dedicated museum-standard exhibition spaces in Scotland (with over 1500 square metres divided into four galleries). First-rate social spaces including excellent places to eat, drink and relax are integral to the concept of the building and to the Waterfront project whose primary aim is to reconnect the city with its river and beautiful views across to Fife.

The vision and drive to achieve this has come about through the V&A at Dundee partnership. This alliance is thoroughly inspiring whether from the perspective of business or design; it is bound to increase visitors and economic and cultural opportunities for the city and wider region. As part of the pre-opening programme for the V&A at Dundee, a major V&A exhibition will be held at the McManus: Dundee's Art Gallery & Museum every autumn until the new building is open.

VandAatDundee.com

Image: James Howie © The Artist's estate

James Howie

Dundee painter James Howie who died in 2011 was one of the great Scottish artists of the last 50 years.

Feted early in his career, the subject of art house documentaries and sought out by art world luminaries, he was only really comfortable in his Dundee studio and the Angus coast painting some of the finest and most evocative landscapes you are ever likely to see. Annoyingly for the growing band of fans who collected his art, Jim (as he was known to his friends) was always a reluctant seller only parting with his beloved work when financial needs must.

He was fiercely loyal to Dundee, walking daily from his house in Peel St with his dog to his studio near the Law and would never hear a word said against it.

He was instrumental in the founding of the Dundee Printmaker's workshop, which now houses state-of-the-art facilities so people can create print, photography and digital work, but he had no time for the pomposity the creative world can be famous for.

Some of Jim's paintings are currently held by public collections in Dundee, and his many fans and admirers would no doubt welcome a major retrospective celebrating his work.

Dundee Contemporary Arts (DCA)

▪ 152 Nethergate, 01382 909900. Gallery opening times: Tue-Sat 11am-6pm; Thu 11am-8pm; Sun noon-6pm.

Since opening in 1999, the DCA has become a favourite venue and meeting place for all generations. The centre combines an excellent gallery and workshop space, a popular café bar (Jute) and a cinema showing arthouse films. Inside, there's a sense of space and sophistication. The conversion of this old warehouse by Richard Murphy Architects has created a light and attractive building in which many different activities can happen at the same time. As well as the two cinemas, there is a print-making studio open to all (often offering low-cost courses), as well as resources for making digital videos. At street level, the angular frontage blends well with the surrounding architecture because of the use of muted colours mixed with copper, glass and wood. Inside, the high ceilings, white walls and large windows make it an enjoyable venue to spend time in. The gallery shows work from major international contemporary visual artists in a series of exhibitions throughout the year. Many visitors head straight downstairs to Jute and the cinemas, making it a bustling venue, particularly on Friday and Saturday nights.
dca.org.uk

Eduardo Alessandro Studios

▪ 30 Gray Street, Broughty Ferry, 01382 737011. Mon-Sat 9.30am-5pm. Closed Sun

This gallery sells contemporary Scottish art, rare and sporting prints and also has as a workshop framing pictures. Well-known local artists sell their work here and it is always worth going along to see the selection of Scottish landscapes.
eastudios.com

Generator Projects

▪ 25-26 Mid Wynd Industrial Estate, 01382 225982. Thu-Sun noon-5pm. Admission free

This space provides an opportunity for unknown artists and art students to show their work. Funded by the Scottish Arts Council and the City Council, it is run by artists and open to everybody. The flexible space is used for making and showing visual art, exhibitions, films and performance.
generatorprojects.co.uk

Hannah Maclure Centre

▪ University of Abertay Dundee, Top Floor, Abertay Student Centre, 1–3 Bell St, 01382 308324. Mon-Fri 9.30am-4.45pm. Admission free

This is an exciting space showing around five exhibitions a year, in addition to displaying projects of staff and students, and hosting other events. It explores the use of new technologies to make artworks and embraces interdisciplinary collaborations. As well as the gallery, where international artists are shown, there is a cinema showing world films, open to the public on Friday afternoons, a cinema club every other Tuesday and a coffee bar.

hannahmaclure centre.abertay.ac.uk

The McManus: Dundee's Art Gallery & Museum

◼ Albert Square, Meadowside, 01382 307200. Mon–Sat 10am–5pm; Sun 12.30–4.30pm. Admission free

The people of Dundee have flocked to the McManus since it reopened. The building and surrounding area benefitted from a four-year refurbishment and reopened in 2010; the new pedestrianised area providing a much improved setting for visitors.

The galleries inside are impressive in a grand Victorian way – the building was designed by Sir Gilbert Scott as a memorial to Prince Albert. In the 19th century, Dundee's jute barons did their civic duty by donating British and European art for the collections and succeeding curators have continued to add modern works, especially those by Scottish artists. The colourists and the Glasgow Boys are well represented and there are some stunning Victorian paintings. The modern gallery spaces have been integrated well with the traditional.

Each gallery has a theme: Landscapes and Lives, for example, includes local archaeology and natural history artefacts, as well as a vivid depiction of the changing flora and fauna over hundreds of years of shifting climate and the settlement of man. Here you'll see a long boat hollowed out from a huge tree. There is something for everyone in here – great paintings, booty from the empire, local history displays, a rare Jacobite flag and the skeleton of the great humpbacked whale which in 1883 dared to swim up the Tay. It was chased northwards by expert Dundee whalers, harpooned to death and later sold at auction for £226. The new café sells coffee and light meals with the added bonus of fine stained glass windows to look at.

mcmanus.co.uk

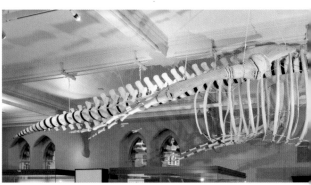

Broughty Castle Museum

■ Castle Approach, Broughty Ferry, 01382 436916. Apr-Sep: Mon-Sat 10am-4pm; Sun 12.30-4pm Oct-Mar: Tue-Sat 10am-4pm; Sun 12.30-4pm. Closed Mon. Admission free

This fortified medieval building is central to this picturesque village overlooking the Tay. Inside, winding stone steps lead to exhibitions on the local area, military history, the colonial era and wildlife. It is fun to climb to the lookout room and take in the excellent views over the Tay, these days spotting dolphins, not warships. The gem here is The Orchar Collection of Scottish Victorian art, which includes paintings by William McTaggart, whose work was immensely successful in his lifetime, and other artists of the Scott Lauder school, depicting mainly genre and rural scenes. There is also a charming painting of a girl by the 20th-century society portraitist, Philip de Laszlo, and a farmyard scene by James McIntosh Patrick. The shop sells postcards and outside there are defences and fortifications to investigate.
dundeecity.gov.uk/broughtycastle

The McManus: Dundee's Art Gallery & Museum The Tay Whale is a great attraction

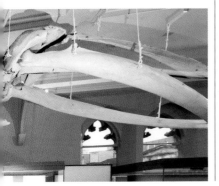

Lorraine Kelly
Lorraine is the Scottish television presenter of *Daybreak* and *Lorraine*. She lives in Broughty Ferry and is an avid Dundee United supporter.

'I was one of the patrons for the refurbishment of the McManus Galleries and it is currently the jewel in Dundee's crown. All the upheaval has been worth it after the biggest facelift in its 138-year history. Locals and visitors alike enjoy seeing Dundee's story told in an educational, inspirational and entertaining way.'

Culture

University Museum Collections Great collection of scientific aids

D'Arcy Thompson Zoology Museum

◼ Carnelley Building, University of Dundee, 01382 384310. Open on Friday afternoons during the summer holidays, otherwise by appointment. Occasional evening lectures and other events, check website for details. Admission free

Sir D'Arcy Wentworth Thompson is best known for his 1917 book *On Growth and Form*, described as the greatest work of prose in 20th-century science. He was the first professor of biology at Dundee and collected a fascinating array of specimens from around the world, which he used for teaching and for his pioneering research into mathematical biology. They are displayed here alongside original charts, models and artworks. **dundee. ac.uk/museum/zoology**

Tayside Medical History Museum

■ Medical School Foyer, Ninewells Hospital, 01382 384310. Open daily 9am-5pm. Admission free.

Exhibits in this intriguing museum include early x-ray equipment, surgical instruments and hospital equipment. Run jointly by the university and NHS Tayside, its permanent displays and temporary exhibitions showcase the rich history of medical excellence in the region, which includes pioneering work in the development of aspirin, radiology, cancer research, keyhole surgery and understanding of allergies. A short walk away in the hospital grounds is the Maggie's Centre, designed by Frank Gehry. Because Maggie's is a centre for cancer patients it is not open to the general public, but the exterior is easy to see and includes an award-winning garden design and a striking Anthony Gormley sculpture. **dundee.ac.uk/museum/ medical.htm**

University Museum Collections

■ University of Dundee, 01382 384310. Galleries open Mon-Fri 9.30am-8.30pm; Sat 9.30am-4.30pm. Admission free

If you are in the city for a longer stay, it is worth visiting these collections, housed in various venues across the campus: there's a fascinating mix of scientific instruments, old teaching aids, textiles, furniture and an impressive art collection including work by former students and staff of Duncan of Jordanstone College of Art & Design. As the university does not have a permanent museum building, there are special exhibitions in the Tower Foyer and Lamb Galleries in the Tower Building and other displays around the campus. Visit the website or call for more information. **dundee.ac.uk/museum**

Scotland's Jute Museum @ Verdant Works

■ West Henderson's Wynd, 01382 309060
verdantworks.com

See Attractions, page 23.

Theatre

Caird Hall

■ City Square, 01382 434940 (box office)
cairdhall.co.uk

See Nightlife, page 78.

Dundee Rep

■ Tay Square, 01382 223530

The theatre that brought us The Proclaimers musical *Sunshine on Leith* is unique in the UK for supporting a permanent ensemble of actors. In 1999, then-director Hamish Glen secured a National Lottery grant to support 14 actors for three years. The scheme was a success and continues

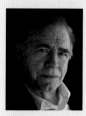

Brian Cox

Brian is an Emmy award-winning stage and film actor. It was recently announced that he will provide the voice for Neil Forsyth's Dundonian character Bob Servant in a BBC radio adaptation of the work.

'The Dundee Rep was really pioneering. It was where I started my theatrical career and developed my interest in acting when I was a teenager. The Rep itself really marked the card for the whole idea of what a rep was. The old building actually burned down but the wreck is still there. In fact, I've been back and found the spot where I used to put up posters.'

to this day. What it means for audiences is more actors on stage and, because of longer rehearsal times, a better standard of production. There is also a pleasure to be had in seeing familiar faces tackling unfamiliar plays. What it means for the actors is the opportunity to hone their skills and develop ties with the resident Scottish Dance Theatre, the community company and the city at large. The 70-year-old company, which gave Brian Cox (left) his first break, offers a broad repertoire of its own in addition to the visiting programme of stand-up comedy, dance and drama. Recent hits have ranged from a powerful production of Edward Albee's *Who's Afraid of Virginia Woolf* to a revival of Scottish dramatist Zinnie Harris's *Further Than the Furthest Thing* – both big winners in the Critics' Awards for Theatre in Scotland, as well as the reliably high quality Christmas show. **dundeerep.co.uk**

The Space

■ Kingsway Campus, Dundee College, Old Glamis Road, 01382 834934.

The Space is a RIBA award-winning multi-purpose venue. Those making the first claim are the students enrolled in the Scottish School of Contemporary Dance, which offers three and four year full-time degree courses and has close ties with Scottish Dance Theatre, the country's leading professional company, based at Dundee Rep. Since the opening of the Space in 2002, the students have been making use of three bright, airy and interlinked dance studios – with their double-height ballet barres – as well as the flexible theatre itself. Flexibility is the 200-seat theatre's strength. As well as performances from the likes of Scottish Ballet and Stephen Petronio, it is used for shows by students on the theatre arts course, who often collaborate with the dance students. The two-floor building with its distinctive curves is also a great facility for Dundee as a whole.
dundeecollege.ac.uk

Dundee Rep

The acclaimed Dundee Rep is entering a new phase of development with artistic director James Brining's impending exit after nine years.

James Brining's soon to be appointed successor should find the Rep in a pretty fit state – it has continued to grow and develop despite the current economic climate, and it is the only arts organisation in the country previously backed by the Scottish Arts Council as a three-year Foundation-funded body to be given a guarantee of a similar status by Creative Scotland over the next three years.

The Rep offers a broad repertoire in addition to its wide ranging visiting programme. Musicals are a feature, with Brining directing Sondheim's *Sweeney Todd* – which won Best Musical at the Theatrical Management Association Theatre Awards. Recently, associate director Jemima Levick directed Robert Harling's *Steel Magnolias*, while Brining's revival of Zinnie Harris's *Further Than the Furthest Thing* was shortlisted for a raft of awards.

There's more change happening at Scottish Dance Theatre, Scotland's national dance company and residents of the Rep, who've recently appointed Fleur Darkin to the role of Artistic Director, a former Associate Artist at Bristol Old Vic and whose recent work, The Blake Diptych, was commissioned by the Southbank Centre **dundeerep.co.uk**

the mcmanus

DUNDEE'S ART GALLERY & MUSEUM

Mon to Sat 10am - 5pm
Sun 12.30 - 4.30pm
Last entry is 15 minutes
before gallery closing time

Admission Free

The McManus:
Dundee's Art Gallery & Museum
Albert Square
Meadowside
Dundee
DD1 1DA

For further information on how to find
McManus, events and facilities please
visit the website or call **01382 307200**.

RECOGNISED

The City's fine art, decorative
art and whaling collections a
recognised as being of nation
significance.

Leisure & Culture Dundee is a
Scottish Charitable Incorporated
Organisation No. SC042421

www.themcmanus-dundee.gov.uk

heritage lottery fund
LOTTERY FUNDED

HISTORIC SCOTLAND

leisure & culture DUNDEE

PROJECT PART-FINANCED
BY THE EUROPEAN UNION
Europe and Scotland
Making it **work together**

esep

Whitehall Theatre

■ 112 Bellfield Street,
08717 029 486

An independent, commercially run theatre in a 1920s art deco building (look out for the murals) which relies on the goodwill of volunteers to supplement the work of the small core staff. Split between 500-seat stalls and 250-seat balcony, the theatre presents a busy bill of popular entertainers, musical favourites, stage comedies, stand-up comedians, larger-scale children's shows and musicals from local amateur dramatics societies as well as the occasional modern dance company. The bright 72-seat

café looks onto the trees in the small grassy square adjacent to the theatre entrance.
whitehalldundee.co.uk

Nesta

Nesta is an independent charity with a mission to help people and organisations bring great ideas to life. Their work is focused on innovation.

Jackie McKenzie, head of Innovation Programmes, manages the Dundee-based team and Nesta's varied work streams in Scotland. She designed and set up Nesta's creative start-up programme Starter for 6, a programme which was adopted by Creative Scotland to support creative businesses in Scotland and is now delivered by the Cultural Enterprise Office in Scotland.

Jackie says: 'We have also run programmes supporting older people to create social enterprises, supporting local authorities to create new digital services for their communities using open data. We are currently running programmes in Scotland: one supporting cultural organisations to use technology to get to new markets and one testing out the potential for 'hyper-local media' on mobile technology. We are pleased that we get to do such wide ranging and interesting work from Dundee. It's a very central location for us – we are an hour away from most of Scotland and can get to other parts of the UK, including London very easily by train or flight.' **nesta.org.uk/ areas_of_work/scotland**

Activities

From gentle city walks
and lively skate parks to
golf and football, Dundee
has a range of activities
for all levels of energy.
The compact nature of the
city means that whatever
activity you want to try out,
it's all within easy reach.
Just get your trainers on
and go.

DUNDEE
ONE CITY, MANY DISCOVERIES

Ancrum Outdoor Education Centre & Clatto Water Sports Centre

■ 10 Ancrum Road, 01382 435911. Opening times and prices vary according to activity

This organisation offers courses in a variety of sports and activities, including blokarting (also known as land karting), climbing, gorgewalking, rafting, sailing, mountain biking and winter sports. The centre runs courses throughout the year as well as offering adventure weeks for children. The instructors are fully qualified and you can hire good quality equipment. The courses often take place in locations such as the Tay and the Glens. The centre has a video and navigation room where it holds preparatory sessions. **ancrum.com**

Avertical World Climbing Centre

■ The Old Church, 7-11 Blinshall Street, 01382 201901. Mon-Fri noon-10pm; Sat/Sun 10am-7pm. Admission variable. Equipment can be hired on site

Situated in an old church, this climbing centre offers abseiling as well as challenging, intermediate and easy routes for all levels of climbing. It provides a broad range of courses for all abilities, holds many competitive events in the winter and allows you to book private and group sessions. Children from age four and above are welcome (along with a proficient adult),

and there is a well-stocked shop with helpful and expert assistants.
averticalworld.co.uk

Balgay Park

■ Balgay Hill

A rich assortment of trees and shrubs and fine views of the Tay make this park a very attractive haven right in the middle of Dundee. There is lots of wildlife here – listen for woodpeckers along the twisting paths which make it feel like a wild space, rather than a municipal park. The recently restored Hird Bridge links the park with Balgay cemetery. Spanning a natural gorge, it was built in 1879, just after the park opened as a recreation ground for mill workers. The park includes Victoria Park, a rose garden and a pitch and putt course as well as the Mills Observatory (page 50).

Battlefield Live Dundee

■ Kingway East Leisure Park, 01382 690820. Mon, Wed-Fri 5-9pm; Sat & Sun noon-9pm

If you are looking for something alternative to do for fun then this is the place to be. An amazing concept where you get the chance to play in your own video game scenario . . . in person! This

Broughty Ferry Beach Golden sands at the mouth of the Tay

indoor gaming centre is very affordable with prices starting from £6. The centre is located to the eastern side of the city with free parking available. Ideal for large groups.
battlefieldlivedundee.co.uk

Baxter Park
■ Stobswell

Baxter Park is one of Dundee's many inner city green spaces. The park is beautifully landscaped with an impressive refurbished pavilion. In the summer Baxter Park attracts people from all parts of the community to enjoy the pleasant surrounds. Probably most known for the spectacular annual firework display. There is also nicely designed community building to the top

Parks and open space

In a city with such an industrial background, it may be surprising to hear that over a quarter of Dundee's urban area is open space of one sort or another, from country parks to local green spaces. Dundee City Council and other agencies recognise that public open spaces contribute a tangible benefit to residents' quality of life, and as such Dundee's green places are well-kept and have a sustainable future within the cityscape. The local community also see this as a priority, and Dundee Trees & Woods in Greenspace (TWIGS) works with everyone within the community to help improve the green environment in and around Dundee City Centre. For a full list of Dundee's parks, see the website.
dundeecity.gov.uk/ environment/parksgardens
■ **Dundee Trees & Woods in Greenspace** dundeetwig.com
■ **Dundee Public Open Space Strategy** dundeecity.gov.uk/ leisurecomms/pos

Bringing in the new

Dundee City Council are nailing their colours to the mast of low carbon renewable energy and at the Michelin Factory site in the Douglas area two 120 metres high wind turbines have turned since 2006. They are rare examples of urban wind turbines.

The deepwater Port of Dundee, which is owned by Forth Ports PLC is a fertile acreage for renewables and relevant support services. In 2011, it was made an Enterprise zone for low carbon and renewables development which gives incentives to companies that invest there. A 60 acre site in the port is the focus of the opportunities for the green energy sector. It is hoped to make the port a hub that will attract the manufacture of offshore wind turbines and a base for the servicing of these renewables. Industrial space at Claverhouse has been made available for the development of a local supply chain.

Although the population of Dundee is under 150,000 people, the surge towards renewables is part of the regeneration of the whole of the Waterfront of Dundee which, under strong governance by the council, is part of the second biggest regeneration project in Scotland and is key to the renaissance of Dundee. It is billed by the press as Dundee's great opportunity, a chance to put behind it forever the shadow cast by Aberdeen when Dundee was turned down as the hub for all the oil investment in the North Sea. The universities of Dundee are also contributing to the strength of this strategy, with specialist courses concentrating on the application and theories of renewable energy. Dundee Renewables is also promoting the Dundee Sun City project, although as yet the council has had to shelve the scheme to put solar panels on all its properties.

While it is likely that individual low carbon technologies will face challenges when operating at scale, there can be no doubt that enormous changes in both energy production and consumption will take place over the next 50 years and Dundee is intent on taking part in the sector. **dundeerenewables.com**

of the park organising many community events. **dundeecity.gov.uk/ environment/baxterpark**

Broughty Ferry Beach
■ Broughty Ferry, four miles east of Dundee city centre

A lovely place for a stroll or serious walk, and only a short bus ride from Dundee city centre. The beach starts close to Broughty Castle and you can walk for miles northwards along the sand, enjoying the great views across the estuary, towards Tentsmuir Point and back towards Dundee. The award-winning Barnhill Rock garden is a nice diversion en route, with some comfortable benches for picnicking. After an afternoon of fresh air and exercise, you could explore the snug little pubs, cafes and craft shops among the attractive old streets and alleyways of this old fishing town.

Camperdown Country Park
■ Coupar Angus Road, 01382 431818; Camperdown Golf Course, 01382 431820; Camperdown House, 01382 431850; Countryside Ranger Service 01382 431848. Admission free

This lovely old estate on the edge of Dundee is a favourite place for walkers and their dogs, covering about 400 acres and housing 190 species of tree. It incorporates Templeton Woods and Clatto Reservoir, linked by paths for those who would like to walk or cycle. Camperdown House is impressive, but it is not open to the public. It was built in 1828 and forms an elegant centrepiece to the park. Keen gardeners will certainly be interested in the mutant Camperdown Elm, from which thousands of grafts have been made. So far it has escaped Dutch elm disease. **camperdownpark.com**

Camperdown Wildlife Centre
■ Coupar Angus Road, 01382 431806. Mar-Sep: Mon-Sun 10am-4.30pm; Oct-Feb: Mon-Sun 10am-3.30pm. Admission £3.50 (adult), conc & child £2.80, kids under 3 £1, family (2 adults 3 kids) £10

An award-winning wildlife centre can also be found at Camperdown. It is a great day out for the family, and the centre has 50 different species of animals, including wolves, brown bears and lemurs. A new visitor centre and cafe opened in summer 2010. **dundeecity.gov.uk/ camperdown/**

Clatto Country Park

■ Dalmahoy Drive, 01382 435911 (for water-based activities) and 01382 436505 for any other query

This was built as a reservoir and now provides a great opportunity for water sports. Back on dry land, beside the water you'll find easy walks, a children's play area and picnicking and barbeque sites. The Ancrum Outdoor Education Centre (see page 42) runs water-based courses here.

Cycling

Dundee is well-equipped with plenty of cycle paths (page 100), and it is easy to hire bikes when visiting (page 107), making pedal power a great way to get around.

Games industry

Dundee has long been at the forefront of gaming technology development. University of Abertay Dundee is a world leader in computer games education, launching the world's first Computer Games Technology degree in 1997; in just over ten years the institution was feeding into the city's fifteen games development studios.

In 2010 the industry was shaken by the collapse of Realtime Worlds, a company founded by the creator of Lemmings and Grand Theft Auto. Over a hundred jobs were lost, and things began to look bleak.

But not for long. Outplay Entertainment, which specialises in mobile and social media games, announced it was setting up its base in Dundee, with the creation of 150 jobs. Later the same year, Dundee played host to 2011's Dare Proto Play games festival, which included the culmination of an international video game design competition.

Add in the Chancellor's 2012 announcement of tax relief for the sector, which industry leaders are hopeful will encourage investment and boost the nation's creative and economic output, and it would seem things can go from strength to strength for Dundee's digital economy.

DISC (Dundee International Sports Complex)

■ Mains Loan, 01382 438804. Mon-Fri 10am-10pm; Sat 10am-6pm; Sun 10am-9pm. Fitness studio opens Mon-Sat from 8am. Admission prices vary

This centre hosts national competitions and runs a variety of fitness classes, and besides the fitness suite it has facilities for five-a-side football, table tennis, bowling, volleyball, netball, and badminton. **dundeecity.gov.uk/sportscentres/ disc.htm**

Downfield Golf Club

■ 01382 825595.

Set in beautiful parkland, Dundee's premier course is a challenge to every golfer teeing off. Downfield is one of the finest inland course in the United Kingdom. Playing host past tournaments like the S.P.G.A. Masters, P.G.A. Scottish Open. You are never more than 25 minutes from Downfield, so don't miss out on adding this great course to your visit. **downfieldgolf.com**

Dundee Botanic Garden

■ Riverside Drive, 01382 381190. Mar–Oct: Mon–Sun 10am–4.30pm; Nov–Feb: Mon–Sun 10am–3.30pm; coffee shop: Mon–Sun 9am–5pm. Admission £3; children £2; senior citizens £2; family (2 adults & 2 children) £8. Entry for university staff and students is free

Swap the hustle and bustle of the city for a slice of tranquillity at Dundee Botanic Garden. The gardens are a spectacular green space with areas for different plant habitats. From the tropical rainforest glasshouse, with banana trees, citrus fruits and a pond with giant water lilies, to Sir Garnet Wilson's sycamore, which was the only tree on site when the garden was started and is named after the lord provost of 1940–46, Dundee Botanic Garden provides year-round enjoyment. Particularly worth a look is the garden of evolution, with its impressive dry stone walls and its explanation of the evolution

Christina Potter
Principal, Dundee College

'I think people really like that within five minutes drive from Dundee they can be out in the beautiful countryside. You've got fantastic views over the Tay and it has its full share of bright, sunny east coast days. Dundee has got a lot of selling points.'

William McNeilly
Age 23

'The people of Dundee really make the city and are good fun to be around.'

Activities

of plants. In the native plant area you can see the variety of plants grown in Scotland. The coffee shop is popular for homemade cakes and soups and the adjacent plant sales area is perfect for a nosey around. The garden sometimes hosts open-air performances, so call ahead for upcoming events. **dundee. ac.uk/botanic/**

Dundee Law
■ Law Road

Dundee Law is an extinct volcano, standing proud above the city. The Law is the city's most distinctive landmark, and for many years was central to Dundee's defences. Once home to an Iron Age fort, it now has a memorial for the two world wars standing at the summit. The Law is most notable for the breathtaking panoramic views it offers. On a clear day, visibility stretches over 45 miles of scenery across the city itself, Fife, the Tay Estuary, Perthshire and the Sidlaw hills. The summit is reachable by car, bike or foot – the steep climb is not for the faint-hearted. Fact panels frame the observation point, offering visitors historical and environmental information and the view at night is mesmerising. The Law is a must-see for visitors and locals to truly appreciate Dundee's unique location.

The Factory Skatepark
■ 15 Balunie Drive, 01382 509586. Mon-Fri 10am-10pm; Sat 9am-8pm; Sun 10am-8pm. Admission £6 for two hours; £3 for beginner sessions

Besides having fabulous

indoor skateboard, roller blade and BMXing facilities, the Factory Skatepark offers basketball, an internet café and an Indian restaurant. For the young and active this is a great venue for all levels of ability. The Factory was purpose-built to give youngsters a well-maintained space to practise in, rather than having to improvise in abandoned buildings. You can enjoy fully supervised beginner sessions, book coaching sessions and hire equipment. There are girls-only sessions to encourage girls to participate. During term-time, the skateboarding runs alongside complementary and often free activities allowing primary school children to combine a supervised homework session with 45 minutes of furious physical activity. Workshops are run on such diverse subjects as graffiti art, healthy lifestyle and photography. Elsewhere in the city Dudhope Park Skatepark is outside, free and open during daylight hours. **factoryskatepark.com**

Golf

There are some excellent golf courses in Dundee (page 99), meaning you don't have to travel far to enjoy a perfect round.

Ice Arena
■ Camperdown Leisure Park, 01382 889369

Perfect for a rainy day, the Ice Arena is well established and award winning. It offers lessons for all ages and public sessions

Football

To some people Dundee is famous for being the city with the two professional clubs with the closest grounds in the UK. When it is said that it is possible to kick a ball out of Dens Park and land it in Tannadice it is barely a lie. So why two clubs? Both Dundee and Dundee United have a proud, long and independent history. Although it is fair to say United have been in the ascendancy in recent times it was not always thus. Dundee's heyday was the 1960s, winning the league in 1962 and getting to the semi-final of the European Cup the next year, a pattern that was repeated by United in the 1980s. Dundee has suffered in recent years from a torrid spell of financial misery but there are signs of better times. Hopefully Dundee will again join the Premier League and the derby will again become one of the highlights of the city's sporting calendar.

■ **Dundee Football Club**, Dens Park Stadium, Sandeman Street, 01382 826104, dundeefc.co.uk

■ **Dundee United Football Club**, Tannadice Park, Tannadice Street, 01382 833166, dundeeunitedfc.co.uk

Louise Smith
CEO, Dundee Science Centre, Sensation

'I took to Dundee immediately. I was amazed at the setting and location – the amount of parkland, green spaces, a feeling of openness and the amazing riverside location, and so much sunshine! I grew up in a small village in the country and couldn't believe that a city could feel so green and open.'

Activities

where equipment can be hired. It also hosts the occasional evening show in a swirl of sequins and disco lights. All of the staff are trained to a very high standard and are happy to help with any queries. The Ice Arena provides a brilliant day out for all ages. **dundeeicearena.co.uk**

Lochee Swim Centre

■ St Mary's Lane, Lochee, 01382 431840. Open every day, times vary according to school term times and holidays. Admission £2.60 (swim only)

This medium-sized swimming pool also has a fitness suite and sauna. **swimlochee.co.uk**

Mills Observatory

■ Glamis Road, Balgay Park, 01382 435967. Apr–Sep: Tue–Fri 11am–5pm; Sat/Sun 12.30–4pm; Oct–Mar: Mon–Fri 4–10pm; Sat/Sun 12.30–4pm

Reach for the stars at the UK's only full-time public observatory. The sandstone building was a gift to the people of Dundee, donated in 1935 by linen manufacturer and keen amateur scientist John Mills. Entry to the observatory is usually free, other than the planetarium shows, which project a simulated night sky onto the domed ceiling, showing thousands of stars and the Milky Way. Two display areas show models and pictures of the solar system in addition to local information and historical equipment – including the original telescope used at the observatory in 1935. The main viewing telescope is upstairs, and there are also a variety of smaller telescopes and binoculars for visitors to use on the viewing balcony. By day, the balcony offers fantastic views of the river and surrounding areas. Mills Observatory appeals to astronomy lovers and novices alike. Part of the Dark Sky Scotland programme. **dundeecity.gov.uk/mills**

Olympia Leisure Centre

■ Earl Grey Place, 01382 432300. Open every day, times vary. Call or check the website for most up to date information. Admission prices vary

DOLPHINS HAVE COME TO THE RIVER IN RECENT YEARS

Olympia Leisure Centre consists of a large fun pool which is very popular with children and families because of its waves, rapids and chutes. There is a baby pool and a training pool for quieter swimming and there's also a fitness suite. At the time of writing, the centre is due to close in 2013, with the new Olympia Leisure Centre already being built at Allan Street, next to Gallacher Retail Park **swimolympia.co.uk**

Soccerworld
■ Old Glamis Road, Dundee;
01382 816888

Whether it's a kickaround with mates or a five-a-side league, Soccerworld caters to all. With eight new pitches of artificial turf, players of all ages and abilities can start perfecting their skills. To make the experience even more Premiership, teams can enter into a league, with prizes to be won each season. A sports bar for parents, showing all major games, keeps everyone happy.
soccerworlduk.com

Swannie Ponds
■ Stobsmuir Park, Pitkerro Road

Popular with locals who come to see the ducks and swans that live happily here and provide plenty of entertainment, the two ponds are surrounded by pathways and beautiful grass banks, daffodils and lots of spring blossom trees. When they get tired of spectators, the birds have a well-planted island to hide in. It is possible to go boating on the ponds. **dundeecity.gov.uk/ environment/stobsmuir**

Tay River Trips & Dolphin watching
■ 01382 562497, Apr-Oct; Taymara 01382 542516. For times and prices see website

These sightseeing and wildlife tours in the Tay Estuary are run by voluntary organisation Taymara, which trains volunteers how to handle a boat safely. The bottlenose dolphins have come to the area in recent years, and no one knows whether they will stay

here permanently. The boats do not chase the dolphins, but their seemingly inquisitive nature means the dolphins often approach the boats of their own accord, bow riding and putting on acrobatic displays. If you don't want to get on a boat, one of the best vantage points for dophin watching is Broughty Castle ramparts.
tayrivertrips.org

Walking in Dundee

Walking is a wonderful way to absorb the character of this city. Dundee has a beautiful riverscape, with views across to Fife, and stretches of it have been developed for walking close to the water. Other places to walk are Balgay Hill and Victoria Park, where there are tall trees, birdsong and flowers, or the Law, a volcanic hill topped with a war memorial. Camperdown Park is generously set with paths and stately trees. You can forget you are in a city there and walk for hours. A visit to Dundee Botanic Garden is a delight, the paths meander around well-planned and well-kept sections, and you can retreat into the glasshouses if the weather turns bad. A short walk around the city centre takes you to the Howff, the ancient burial ground given to the city by Mary Queen of Scots. The gravestones give a great insight into the occupations of the people over centuries.

Shop

With a proud tradition of independent traders, Dundee has an inspiring mix of shops of all sizes, making for a vibrant city centre. Coffee merchants, sporting supplies, a kitsch tartan tea cosy and designer brands – you can find them all within a few steps of the Overgate and Wellgate shopping centres.

DUNDEE
ONE CITY, MANY DISCOVERIES

Arkive

■ 36-40 Seagate, 01382 206615. Mon-Sat 9.30am-6pm; Sun noon-5pm

Formerly Ozzy's, now Arkive, this large, bright shop is a self-confessed 'lifestyle store'. With high fashion and street style, Arkive caters for everyone from preppy to skater. An open-plan shop floor is staffed by assistants happy to help you negotiate your way from Diesel to Carhartt; G Star to DCs. The Boardroom sells skate gear and accessories, with some exclusive brands, as well as a spray paint section for street artists and art students. There is a sizeable female section providing funky hoodies, dresses and a rainbow of skinny jeans. Accessories such as Skull Candy headphones and surfer-style necklaces are scattered around the shop's nooks and crannies. With such a wide range of fashions, it is difficult to find fault with this on-trend store. **ozzys.co.uk**

Big Bairn Books

■ 17 Exchange Street, 01382 220225. Tue-Sat 10.45am-4.45pm. Closed Sun & Mon

This Aladdin's cave of Dundee's literary history specialises in annuals and comics from DC Thomson, the publishers of *The Beano*, *The Dandy*, *Oor Wullie* and *The Broons*, as part of a quiet celebration of the place that added journalism to Dundee's three Js. The shop also offers classic Scottish literature and a selection of second-hand books. Come in to while away time in this hidden gem.

The Cheesery

■ 9 Exchange Street, 01382 202160. Tue-Fri 9.30am-5.30pm; Sat 9.30am-5pm. Closed Sun

Since opening in January 2008, Dorothy Hegarty's delightful wee cheese shop (the first of its kind in the city) has been quick to make its mark, winning Dundee Retail Awards' Newcomer of the Year, and quickly gathering many regular customers. There are over 50 cheeses, 20 from the British Isles, the most local being the Anster from St Andrews. The southern beauties hail from the likes of Snowdonia and Cornwall, while among the continental cheeses you will find the unashamedly smelly Epoisses from Burgundy. The Cheesery is also a great showcase for other local produce – handmade oatcakes from Cupar and Carnoustie, ceramics from St Andrews and many preserves and chutneys. If you're looking for a wedding cake with a difference, Dorothy can supply you with a magnificent tiered 'cheese' cake, made up of whole wheels of differing sizes of cheese. Bright and welcoming. **thecheesery.co.uk**

DCA Shop

■ 152 Nethergate, 01382 909900. Mon-Sat 10.30am-5.30pm; Thur 10.30am-8.30pm; Sun noon-4.30pm

This design shop is possibly the best of its kind in Scotland. With one side being entirely glazed, this light and airy space creates the perfect showcase

Fisher and Donaldson Baking daily treats for hungry Dundonians

for the finest contemporary design. The high-quality, innovative work on sale includes jewellery, textiles and ceramics both decorative and practical. It's encouraging to see such a strong focus on home-grown creative production together with other UK and international designers and makers. You will also find highly desirable household goods from larger design companies such as Marimekko, and Joseph Joseph, select stationery goods, greeting cards and art magazines. For children, there's a great range of unusual toys and craft projects, while kids' books by local illustrators can be found among the thoughtfully stocked staircase bookshelf. The staff are helpful and knowledgeable about the represented designers and artists, and can advise those on a tighter budget about their 'Own Art' scheme, which makes investing in a beloved piece of art or design more affordable. **dca.org.uk/shop/index.html**

Fisher and Donaldson

■ 12 Whitehall Street, 01382 223488. Branches also at 300 Perth Road, and 83 High Street, Lochee. Mon-Sat 8am-5.15pm. Closed Sun

Everyone loves a bun, and some of the finest to be found in these parts are at this fourth-generation family bakery. Alongside the essential Dundee cake and its award-winning British apple pie, Fisher and Donaldson also bakes sumptuous wedding cakes. Whether a coffee tower or a steak bridie whets your appetite, the cheery staff are on hand to help. If you have trouble choosing, its in-house café is the perfect place to sample some tasty treats. **fisheranddonaldson.com**

Fraser's Fruit and Veg

■ 300a Perth Road, 01382 669613. Mon- Fri 10am-6pm; Sat 9am-5pm.

Within the small high street area of Perth Road, Fraser's Fruit and Veg attracts customers from all over the city. Prided on locally sourced produce as well as ordering in special for clients from as far as Asia. There is a very local atmosphere in the shop just like visiting the local village grocer. Their ready to go soup bags have been very well received, offering a bi-weekly choice. **frasersfruitandveg. co.uk**

The Gentleman's Groom Room

■ 42 Whitehall Crescent, 01382 801504.

The Gentleman's Groom Room – Classic Grooming for Modern Man. Situated in the southern part of the city centre this retail outlet sells all a man could need for quality grooming. Luxury complementary therapies and treatments, including facials and massages, are available from professionally trained staff. Perfect for special gifts or to kick start a healthier skin regime. **thegentlemansgroomroom. com**

Gows

■ 12 Union Street, 01382 225427. Mon-Sat 9am-(just before) 5pm. Closed Sun

Gows certainly caters for a niche market but is well established in Dundee, trading since 1860 and stocking almost everything the field sport enthusiast could ever need, from guns and binoculars to rods and waterproofs. The staff at Gows are very knowledgeable about their subject and will advise customers unsure of what to purchase. If you are especially interested in fly fishing, it's worth visiting to see their large stock. **gows-secureshop.co.uk**

G&A Spink

■ 10-12 Castle Street, 01382 731493

Famous for their Arbroath smokies G&A Spink is always a popular place for the people of Dundee. The delicatessen boasts fresh produce in fish and seafood. Their mussels are a standout option. The staff are great at giving advice on what produce would suit your pallet. So don't be bamboozled with the huge range of delicious things on offer.

Grant's Butchers

■ 187 Blackness Road, 01382 669 556. Mon-Sat 7.30am-5.30pm. Closed Sun

The walls of awards bear testimony to the quality and popularity of Grant's Butchers. An important part of the community since 1875, with a knowledgeable staff of just ten people to cater to their ever-growing range of clients, Grant's provides many local businesses as well as a steady flow of regulars. With beef, pork and lamb sourced

THE GROOM ROOM IS PERFECT FOR SPECIAL GIFTS

Shop

from Scotch Premier Meat, Inverurie, it projects a sense of pride in the produce. This is reflected in its Scottish Federation of Meat Trades awards, from the sublime – its pork, cheese and chive burgers, to the ridiculous – the curry-inspired lamb bhuna bangers. Another local favourite is the Balmoral Chicken – neat parcels of chicken fillets stuffed full of haggis. As well as freshly sourced meat, a selection of convenience foods – pots of soup, stew, steak stir-fry, and apple and fruit tarts are made fresh daily.

Groucho's

■ 132 Nethergate, 01382 228496. Mon-Sat 9am-5.30pm; Sun noon-4.30pm

To many a Dundonian, Groucho's is like a much-loved friend. It's moved around a bit since opening in 1976, but seems to have settled down at the foot of the Nethergate. Run by Alastair 'Breeks' Brodie, Groucho's still calls itself a 'disc and tape exchange'. It's the perfect place to adopt your very own Nick Cave or Nat King Cole – most tastes are catered for. Dedicated to public service, Groucho's once had a Bay City Rollers amnesty, where customers could bring in their offending vinyl and smash it in a special box. It was very popular. As you breathe in the comforting aroma of faded record sleeves, you can immerse yourself in a sea of musical genres, browsing through endless CD racks, boxes of vinyl, DVDs and 7" singles – with anything from Patti Smith to Patsy Cline. Groucho's is also a concert ticket agency for gigs around the country and runs buses to some larger events.

For local gigs and club nights, info is posted on the notice board, or in flyer racks. Breeks and his knowledgeable staff will always try their best to help with even the strangest requests – check out the 'Don't Ask' section on the shop's website with choice words from people 'two tracks short of a single'. This undeniable city treasure has deservedly won the Dundee Independent Retailer of the Year for the last two years. Happy browsing. **grouchos.co.uk**

G&A Spink World-famous Arbroath Smokies

Hue - Art, Fashion and Tattoos

■ 30 South Tay Street. Mon-Wed & Fri 10am-5pm; Thur 10am-6pm; Sat 10am-3pm.

Also situated in the cultural quarter Hue's has a very strong art principle at the core of all their works, from custom made to order shoes and one off vintage produce to tattoos. This very professional studio cares a lot for quality and the art. Famous clients have included Danny, Tommy and Dougie from McFly.

Indigo House

■ 69 Perth Road, 01382 206726. Mon/Tue & Thu/Fri 10.30am-5.30pm; Sat 10.30am-5pm. Closed Wed & Sun

Full of curios from owner Ian Smith's travels, Indigo House is a treasure trove. Each find is innovative, recycled and natural, from hand-engraved turquoise and moonstone to Tagua jewellery made from nuts. Scarves, sequinned cushions and ornaments are scattered through the shop, which smells wonderful thanks to the scented candles and incense. The perfect boutique for something a bit special.
indigohouseonline.co.uk

JA Braithwaite Ltd

■ 6 Castle Street, 01382 322693. Mon–Fri 9am–5.30pm; Sat 9am–5pm. Closed Sun

Braithwaite's has been trading since the 19th century, and walking through the door feels like stepping back in time. The tiny tea and coffee merchants is filled with wonderful smells, while the wood panelling on the walls is decorated with coffee sacking and black-and-white photographs of the shop's long history. The staff are quick to welcome customers like old friends and their cheery manner is infectious. For coffee novices, information about the different blends is on hand. Braithwaite's roasts its own beans on the premises using a secret age-old method. In addition to the many varieties of coffee bean, which are weighed out on old, traditional brass scales, Braithwaite's also sells old-fashioned tea tins, mugs and coffee grinders. The wooden floor creaks and the lighting is dim, giving the shop a worn, much-loved feel. Well worth a visit.

FAMOUS CLIENTS HAVE INCLUDED THE BOYS FROM MCFLY

Maggie's Farm Boutique

■ 22 Union Street, 01382 228 447. Mon-Sat 10am-5pm. Closed Sun

Since this little boutique opened almost two years ago, Maggie's Farm has gone from strength to strength. Named after the Bob Dylan song, Maggie's Farm stocks brands from London, as well as hand-picked, remodelled vintage clothing and jewellery. They've also started stocking a line of new, vintage style furniture and have a concession in the Edinburgh branch of Topshop.

Shop

Fraser's Fruit and Veg Great selection of fresh, healthy produce

Shop

Manifesto
■ 78 Commercial Street, 01382 201527. Mon-Sat 10am-5pm. Closed Sun

Manifesto provides one of Dundee's few truly designer clothes shops, offering on-trend clothing from the newest lines available. Its clothes are aimed mainly at the fashion-conscious young professional, both male and female, and the price tags mean students are definitely not the main customer base. It boasts a diverse range of casual clothes by labels including Paul Smith, Armani, Adidas and Replay Jeans. Pay a visit if the usual high street shops are failing to inspire you.

McIntyres
■ 50 Union Street, 121 Perth Road, 01382 202030. Mon/Fri 9am-6pm; Tues-Thur 9am-8pm; Sat 9am-4pm.

McIntyres Salons are Dundee's largest independent hairdressing salon providing a complete range of hairdressing services to a varied male and female clientele. A positive and friendly creative environment designed to achieve the best possible results. Kay McIntyre, artistic director has been a British Hairdressing Award finalist three times. Staff are welcoming and make you feel at home. **mcintyres.co.uk**

McManus Shop
■ Albert Square, 01382 307200. Mon-Sat 10am-5pm, Sun; 12.30-5pm

The McManus is newly refurbished and an unmissable part of any visit to Dundee. To fully appreciate the shop, you really should browse after a tour round the galleries (page 32). It features books on local history, but the impact of the wartime memorabilia and replica items will be lost if you have not visited the exhibitions. **mcmanus.co.uk**

Missy La La's

■ 6 Crichton Street, 01382 220923. Mon-Sat 10am-5.30pm

Stocking clothing and accessories for the young and fashion-conscious woman, Missy La La's offers pieces with a definite designer twist, but still at high street prices. As the exclusive Dundee stockists for a number of lines, it is a refreshing change from the usual suspects. If you fancy sourcing something quirky for your next party, night out or even something different to wear to work, head down here for something you won't find elsewhere. **missylalasboutique.co.uk**

Neo Design Shop

■ 17 Whitehall Cr, 01382 206 658. Mon-Sat 10am-5pm.

Just down the hill from the Overgate is this lovely shop selling locally made jewellery. Details about where, who and how each item was made gives a really nice personal touch to the place. The stylish, contemporary jewellery boutique is acclaimed for housing some of Europe's most exciting work.

Overgate

■ 01382 314200. Mon–Wed & Fri/Sat 9am–6pm, Thu 9am–7.30pm, Sun noon–5pm

Dundee's newest shopping centre boasts a vast range of shops and eateries. The single-sided mall (the only one in Europe) is flanked by an impressive two-storey curved glass wall, which floods the centre with natural light.

Reopened in its present form in 2000, the Overgate has brought high-end retailers to the city. Shops represented include department store Debenhams, which sprawls over three floors, as well as high street favourites French Connection, Primark, Office, Gap, Mango, Lush and a bling-tastic Swarovski boutique. Cafés such as Starbucks and Millie's Cookies provide a welcome break from shopping. **overgate.co.uk**

Rattbags

■ 12 Exchange Street, 01382 223422. Tue-Sat 10.30am- 5pm.

Located in the curious old streets of the town behind the Caird Hall, Rattbags is an equally curious and chic boutique, mainly dealing in quality brand name handbags like Suzy Smith. Also on offer is a range of gorgeous handmade jewellery created by the owner. There is a discount available to students. If you want to treat yourself to something unique then Rattbags is for you. **rattbags.co.uk**

Scarlet Bakery

■ 292 Perth Road, 01382 250066. Mon 10am-5pm; Wed-Sat 10am-5pm.

The Scarlet Bakery is not like your traditional bakery on the Perth Road. Whilst still offering a host of sumptuous cakes to indulge in, there is an interesting twist. Training courses are available for those wanting to brush up on skills in baking and decorating. Priding themselves on the 'wow' factor, Scarlet Bakery

Groucho's Simply a Dundee institution for those into good music

is a friendly place offering goodies of a high standard. **thescarletbakery.com**

Scottish Antiques and Arts Centre

■ Abernyte, Perthshire, 01828 686401. Mon-Sun 10am-5pm

The Scottish Antiques and Arts Centre is a good destination for an afternoon out of the city. Surrounded by beautiful countryside, the substantial centre stocks an eclectic mix of antiques and locally made gifts, including some one-off jewellery pieces and glasswork, as well as soaps and toiletries. The café serves lunches and refreshments and all staff are happy to help with any queries. **scottish-antiques.com**

Scott Brothers Butcher

■ 32 Nethergate, 01382 201342. Mon-Sat 9am-5pm

For nearly 80 years Scott Brothers butchers, poulterers and delicatessen, have been serving satisfied customers in Dundee. With the new city centre store selling locally sourced produce, knowledgeable and friendly staff are on hand to guide you through the great selection of meats. Customers can enjoy good old-fashioned service but know that the most uptodate techniques and controls are in place. **scottbros.co.uk**

Stephen Henderson the Jeweller

■ 1 Union Street, 01382 221339. Mon-Sat 10am-5pm

A huge range of big-name jewellery and watches is available from Stephen Henderson. Its tagline is 'whatever it takes' and it prides itself on its team of dedicated and friendly staff. It also serves hot drinks in the winter, or a cold beer or champagne in the summer to help lubricate your decisions. If you are serious about buying some top-end jewellery in Dundee, this is definitely the place to visit. **stephenhenderson.co.uk**

Sutherlands

■ 90 Nethergate, 01382 224709. Mon-Sat 9am-5.30pm; Sun (Nov & Dec only) noon-4pm

Whereas our capital city is strewn with Scottish shops, Dundee has just the one, but it's a belter. Around for 90 years, and occupying the same spot on Nethergate for over 50 of them, Sutherlands aims to please all. Half of the shop is devoted to the more kitsch side of Scotland, with haggis money banks and Rabbie Burns napkins. The more traditional side offers full highland outfits and kilt accessories, and drinking vessels such as the hip flask or quaich. For the ladies, a fine range of tartan skirts and shawls, and for the bairns, how about a Scotty dog bib? Sutherlands also has a good range of jewellery, all with a Scottish theme, the thistle being a popular motif. There are other places in town to buy a kilt, but no other where you can choose between a Glengarry and a 'See You Jimmy' bunnet. Here's to the next 90 years.

This Little Piggy

■ 185 Brook Street, Broughty Ferry, 01382 770481. Mon-Fri 9am-5pm; Sat 9.30am-5.30pm

With the shop front decked out in a bright Liquorice Allsorts theme, This Little Piggy is child-friendly from the get-go. Indoors, shelves of funky footwear flank a large communal sofa. Spring/summer stock includes cool Geox trainers at the forefront for boys and a line of cute Lelli Kelli sandals for girls. As well as the newest in kids' shoes, jackets and fleeces for the outdoors, it stocks fluffy puppets for younger children. **little-piggy.co.uk**

Tiso

■ 22 Whitehall Street, 01382 221153. Mon, Tue, Fri, Sat 9.30am-5.30pm; Wed 10am-5.30pm; Thur 9.30am-6.30pm. Sun 11am-5pm

Tiso is a Scottish outdoor activity specialist in the heart of the city centre. The spacious store stocks high end brands like Northface and Rab, catering for every need in hiking, outdoor climbing,

travel, camping, and mountaineering. All staff are trained to a high level so you can be sure of good sound advice when you go visit. **tiso.com**

Wellgate Shopping Centre

■ The Wellgate, 01382 225454. Mon–Sat 9am–5.30pm, Sun 11am–5pm

Dundee's 'other shopping centre', the Wellgate, lacks the shiny newness of Overgate but is not to be dismissed. It hosts a range of decent shops including Bhs, New Look and Claire's Accessories. The food court upstairs is hardly gourmet dining but is great for a quick bite to eat. Dundee Central Library (page 19) is situated at the back of the building, where the centre also backs onto Hilltown – one of Dundee's oldest areas, currently in the process of regeneration. **wellgatedundee.co.uk**

Westport Gallery

■ 48 Westport, 01382 221751. Mon–Sat 9am–5pm. Closed Sun

A sophisticated Aladdin's cave, Westport Gallery sells an array of arty pieces. A variety of prints and pictures are available at the gallery, including amazing digital shots and paintings of the bridges over the Tay and other Dundee landmarks. The rest of the shop is stuffed with vases, ornate decorations, lamps, lighting and unique pieces of furniture. Clothes shop Diva is connected to the shop, selling dresses and shirts. With prices spanning all budgets, it's definitely worth a visit. **wpgal.co.uk**

Dorothy Hegarty
The Cheesery

'Dundee means Home Sweet Home! When you've been away for any length of time and you reach the Tay Bridge you know you're back where you belong. Its geographical aspect makes it a very welcoming City – I am proud of its physical vista, its personality and the people that make it this way.

The droll sense of humour in Dundee is unique. The people of the city have an unwavering ability to pick themselves up, dust themselves down and start all over again. Not a day goes by when I don't have a good laugh with a fellow Dundonian.'

Shop

Eat & Drink

After all that sightseeing, what better way to recharge than going out for a friendly drink and enjoyin g a great meal? Dundee has a variety of exciting places to eat, from traditional bakers to contemporary cuisine. With plenty of options you might find yourself spoilt for choice.

DUNDEE
ONE CITY, MANY DISCOVERIES

The Blue Marlin Cape Cod style interior with delicious seafood

Agacan
■ 113 Perth Road, 01382 644227, Tue-Sat 5-9.30pm. Closed Sun/Mon.

Named after its flamboyant owner, this idiosyncratic wee place is rammed with regularly changing local artists' works. The food is uncomplicated, carefully prepared and served up in large portions to eat in or takeaway. Main courses are dominated by kebabs, the sis kofte (minced lamb) and pirzola (lamb cutlets) being the tastiest bets. Wash it down with Turkish beer or wine, and finish with honeyed baklava and eye-popping Turkish coffee.

Anatolia
■ 91 Nethergate, 01382 204857, Mon-Sun 5-10pm

A Dundee institution, Anatolia has been serving hearty Turkish cuisine to hungry customers for over ten years – and it's still BYOB. The portions are generous, with the hummous, lamb and meze platters particularly recommended. It's quite cosy inside so

busy Saturday nights can be atmospheric, but it all adds to the Anatolia experience.

Bellini
■ 36 Commercial Street, 01382 205 444, Mon-Sat noon-2pm, 5-10pm; Sun noon-2pm, 5-9.30pm.

Formerly known as 'The Italian', this family run restaurant has a touch of bling to its décor, and is equally happy with a table of two or a lively party. The long, locally sourced menu has some more unusual dishes like stinco di prosciutto – ham shank with roast potatoes and sauerkraut, as well as good veggie and gluten-free choice. **bellinidundee.co.uk**

The Blue Marlin
■ Camperdown Street, 01382 221397, Mon-Sat noon-2pm, 5.30-9pm. Closed Sun.

After a move to Dundee's up and coming City Quay, the lack of sea views are made up for with fish imagery aplenty, beach-hut panelling and posh-terrace-style sofas giving a Cape

Eat & Drink

Cod holiday vibe. From simple grilled dishes to international flavours, sticking to seafood doesn't mean limiting choice. Prices are high, but good value lunch and early bird menus increase accessibility.
thebluemarlin.co.uk

Bon Appetit
■ 22-26 Exchange Street, 01382 809000, Mon-Thu noon-2pm, 5-9.30pm; Fri/Sat noon-2pm, 5-10.30pm. Closed Sun.

With its simple, café-like furnishings, Bon Appetit has all the ambience and charm of a Left Bank bistro. Service is quick, but the attitude is slow and indulgent. Everything, except the Luvians ice-cream from Cupar and the Scottish cheese platter, is prepared on site, and they're dedicated to local food. You can pre-order online, good for large groups or pre-theatre dining.
bonappetit-dundee.com

Bridgeview Station
■ Riverside Drive, 01382 660066, Sun-Tue 8am-5pm; Wed-Sat 8am-8pm.

Housed in a beautifully converted Victorian railway station right on Dundee's waterfront, the views over the Tay are just part of this café-restaurant's appeal. Bridgeview is a charming place for everything from snacks to full dinners. The 'gastrocafé' menu gives simple international flavours to Scottish ingredients, and a takeaway operation is also available from an 1870s railway carriage outside.
bridgeviewstation.com

Bruach Bar
■ 328 Brook Street, Broughty Ferry, 01382 739878

A short step from Broughty Ferry station, Bruach has a downstairs bar with a name for its cocktails and upstairs restaurant serving decent bar meals. A contemporary vibe comes from cool purple lighting and dark wooden panelling, while dishes like pork belly with black pudding mash give it a slightly formal edge in the evenings. Spectacularly cheap set menus make it a regular rather than special occasion option.
bruachbar.com

Byzantium
■ 11 Hawkhill, 01382 221946, Wed-Sat noon-3pm, 5-10.30pm; Sun noon-10.30pm.

Smart and stylish in the West End's cultural quarter, slate walls, stone floors and lots of glass make this Mediterranean restaurant feel cosmopolitan and a bit special. Flourishes like blood orange jelly and lemon caviar pearls lift the menus out of the ordinary, as do playful touches like the 'Fun at the Fair' sharing dessert, which includes homemade candy floss and baby toffee apples.
byzantiumrestaurant.com

Café Sicilia
■ 123 Perth Road, 01382 665 454, Mon-Thu 9am-6pm; Fri/Sat 9am-9pm; Sun 10am-5pm

A popular local Italian café/bistro focused on homemade pasta and stone-baked pizzas. The interior is somewhat plain,

but the generously sized cakes are baked on site and served with excellent coffee – try the cannoli, a Sicilian sweet pastry, or the ricotta tart. Friday and Saturday are late opening nights, when the full menu comes into its own.
cafesicilia.co.uk

Ciao Sorrento

■ 89 Nethergate, 01382 221760, Tue-Sun 5-10pm; Fri/Sat noon-2pm, 5-10pm; Sun 5-9.30pm.

Joanna Milano has run this traditional Italian restaurant for 15 years. With just 36 covers and a family friendly attitude it has a cheerfully informal vibe which stretches to the simply prepared meals – calamari fritti, insalata caprese and long pizza and pasta lists hold no surprises, though, more unusually, there's also a large range of locally sourced veal dishes.
ciaosorrentodundee.co.uk

Dil'se

■ 99-101 Perth Road, 01382 221501, Mon-Fri noon-2pm, 5-11pm; Sun noon-11.30pm.

Family-run Dil'se has been established in the university

quarter of Dundee for almost a decade. A classic Indian menu is tinged with multiple influences from Afghanistan to Sri Lanka, including a small Thai section, and is also available for takeaway or delivery. Copious linen gives the large, modern restaurant an air of formality and it has a touch more 'special occasion' to it than most Indian joints.
dilse-restaurant.co.uk

Dr Noodles

■ 89 Nethergate, 01382 322 155, Mon-Thu 11am-9pm; Fri/Sat 11am-10pm; Sun noon-9pm.

Part of an expanding chain that includes a second Dundee bar in Fat Sam's, the simple concept includes 60 noodle combinations, none of which will set you back more than £5.50. With takeaway, home delivery or sitting in the contemporary, diner-style restaurant all options, it might not be fine dining but it's certainly a problem solver.
drnoodles.co.uk

Encore Bar & Brasserie

■ Dundee Rep Theatre, Tay Square, 01382 206699, Mon-Sat noon-3pm, 5-9pm. Closed Sun.

Partially closed off from the busy theatre, the buzz remains with the upstairs café open to the theatre crowd, the downstairs restaurant a little quieter. Open all day for coffee and the papers, but closed on non-show evenings, Mediterranean-influenced menus encompass quick and simple (generously sized) snacks and substantial meals, complimented by an imaginative and reasonably **encoredundee.co.uk**

Fishermans Tavern
■ 10-16 Fort Street, Broughty Ferry, 01382 775941, Sun-Wed 11am-midnight; Thu-Sat 11-1am.

A row of 17th century fishermen's cottages is now today's traditional, comfy pub. Daily changing cask ales and good bar food can be enjoyed in the privacy of an alcove, or the beer garden. The only tavern to have featured annually in the Good Beer Guide since 1975, they host a charity beer festival each May, showcasing the area's beers, lagers and ales. **fishermanstavern.co.uk**

Henry's Coffee House
■ 22-26 Seagate, 01382 200225, Mon-Sat 8am-7pm; Sun 10am-7pm. Also opening at 5 City Square

A smart, aspirational newcomer to the Seagate area, this family-run coffee shop has its sights on expansion, with a City Square branch just opened. Regular live music afternoons have carved it a niche, bolstered by reasonable prices, an alcohol licence and a commitment to excellent coffee. Food is lunch staples and cakes, and it's large enough to take advantage of the free wifi without feeling pressured for time. **henryscoffeehouse.co.uk**

Jute Café
■ 152 Nethergate, 01382 909 246, Mon-Sat 10am-4pm, 5-9.30pm; Sun noon–4pm, 5-8.30pm.

Housed in the Dundee Contemporary Arts centre, the massive, airy bar area takes on a number of roles throughout the day, from chilled-out, kid-friendly café during daylight hours to bustling style bar at night. Fish and vegetarian options feature strongly on menus as widely appealing as the place itself, and the outdoor patio is a summer favourite. **dca.org.uk**

Eat & Drink

Bon Appetit Dedicated to sourcing fresh local produce

Bridgeview Station A beautiful setting for some quality food

Malabar

■ 304 Perth Road, 01382 646888, Tue-Sun 5.30-10pm. Closed Mon.

Malabar specialises in southern, particularly Keralan, Indian dishes. While many of the curries will be familiar (and the menu is predominantly curries), it's rarer to see konju – prawns in coconut, varutha meen (pan fried spiced fish) or spiced chicken livers. A small and slightly scruffy restaurant, it's nevertheless popular for its fresh food, generous portions and relaxed ambience.
malabardundee.com

Mandarin Garden

■ 44 South Tay Street, 01382 227 733, Mon-Fri noon-2pm, Sun-Thu 5-11pm, Fri & Sat 5-11.30pm

Tucked away but close to the theatre and DCA, Mandarin Garden is reliable and reasonably priced, with an extensive menu featuring a few unusual items such as lettuce dumplings, as well as the usual favourites like Peking Duck. The atmosphere is friendly and busy with prompt service.

Marco Polo

■ 42 Dock Street, 01382 221811, Mon-Thu, Sun noon-10pm; Fri/Sat noon-10.30pm.

In the hub of Dundee's waterfront development, recently opened Marco Polo offers fusion food worthy of its namesake's travels. Predominantly Mediterranean menus draw influence from the Middle East and Asia, with dishes ranging from beetroot-cured salmon to Mongolian lamb. With contemporary decor and mid-to-high prices, Marco Polo slots perfectly into Dundee's most up-and-coming quarter.
marcopolocuisine.co.uk

Metro Bar and Brasserie

■ Apex City Quay Hotel & Spa, 1 West Victoria Dock Road, 0845 365 0002, Mon-Sun noon-2.30pm; 6-9.30pm

Overlooking Victoria Dock, Metro is bright and stylish, making the most of sea views with wall-length windows. Menus are reasonably priced with a number of set deals, and cater considerably for all eventualities – even baby food isn't forgotten. Good local and Scottish ingredients are taken advantage of in dishes like Glenisla estate game and green peppercorn terrine.
apexhotels.co.uk

Papa Joe's

■ 15 Whitehall Street, 01382 202520, Mon-Sun noon-10.30pm.

An informal, family friendly restaurant, Papa Joe set up his first café in Scotland in 1933. There are now three Joe's across Stirling, Dundee and Dunfermline, each serving an uncomplicated Italian-Mexican-US menu of rib-sticking classics including baby back ribs, pizza, pasta and burgers amongst 1950s Americana décor.
papa-joes.co.uk

The Parlour Café

■ 58 West Port, 01382 203588, Mon-Fri 8am-7pm; Sat 8am-5pm; Sun 9.30am-3pm.

A tiny whitewashed rough brick place with only twenty seats, the Parlour Café is nonchalantly trendy. It's extremely popular with the uni's art students, drawn by the healthy range of toasties and speciality sandwiches, and the regular exhibitions and events. Mostly vegetarian food with international flavours but a strong local conscience, there's a great choice of locally baked cakes.

The Piccolo

■ 210 Perth Road, 01382 201419, Tue-Thu 5.30-9pm; Fri/Sat 5.30-9.30pm. Closed Mon/Sun.

Five minutes from the city centre, Piccolo's small interior manages to be both calming and a touch jazzy, with its witty disco ball and gentle cream tones. The Italian menu is, like the décor, full of comforting but stylish classics, cooked with fresh local ingredients including Spinks fish. Dundee wine merchants Aitken put together the wine list, or you can BYO. **piccolodundee.co.uk**

The Playwright

■ 11 Tay Square, 01382 223113, Mon-Sat noon-3pm, 5pm-6.30pm, 7-9.30pm. Closed Sun.

Offering some of the most inventive fine dining in Dundee, with a price list to match, The Playwright is successfully ambitious. For budget visits go for the lunch or pre-theatre set menus, though you'll miss out on the likes of halibut with crab cannelloni. Around 100 wines and champagnes are available by the bottle, with occasional wine dinners organised to provide a guiding light.
theplaywright.co.uk

Foodie's delight

Dundee may be known for its eponymous fruit cake, but the city's food scene is making a name for itself too. There is an abundance of quality local produce on offer, and a thriving cake and café scene.

Fine local products can be found at places like The Cheesery, which sells quality regional and continental artisan cheeses alongside complementary chutneys, jams and oatcakes. Scottish beef, pork, lamb and venison can be found at a number of local butchers, including Scott Brothers and Grants.

To satisfy a sweet tooth pop into T Ann Cake, an independent bakeshop and café that offers a dizzying variety of homemade cakes, from straightforward scones and tarts to the more out-there chocolate and bacon brownies.

For a more traditional patisserie offering there are three Dundee branches of family bakery Fisher and Donaldson, each offering a selection of breads, pastries and cakes. Goodfellow & Steven, based at Broughty Ferry but with branches all over the city, is another local baker providing a great selection of goodies to Dundonians.

And then of course there is the monthly Dundee Farmers' Market – every 3rd Saturday of the month, the High Street is filled with the finest locally sourced produce, including cheeses, baked goods, meat, jams, and fresh fruit and veg.

■ **dundeecity.gov.uk/citydevelopment/economicdev/ farmersmarket**

■ **t-ann-cake.blogspot.co.uk/**

■ **thecheesery.co.uk/**

■ **fisheranddonaldson.com**

■ **goodfellowscakes.co.uk**

■ **scottbros.co.uk/**

Rama Thai
■ 32-34 Dock Street, 01382 223366, Mon-Sun noon-2pm, 5-10pm.

With its elaborate furnishings, a temple-themed bar and carved artworks, Dundee's first Thai restaurant brings an exotic flavour to the city, and one that has proved very popular. The long, mostly traditional menu has an excellent vegetarian selection and some good lunch deals. Interesting curries like gaeng ped pedyang, with grapes and roast duck, keep things lively. **rama-thai.co.uk**

Rancho Pancho
■ 16 Commercial Street, 01382 229518, Mon-Fri, Sun 5-9.30pm; Sat noon-2pm, 5-9.30pm.

This spirited chain has branches in Perth, Wellbank and right in the centre of Dundee. The colourful, crowd-pleasing menu has a couple of wild cards like prawn ceviche among the fajitas, tacos and enchiladas, and portions are huge. Margaritas are their thing on the drinks front, though the Mexican beer list adds an authentic touch. **ranchopancho.com**

Robertson of Broughty Ferry
■ 234 Brook Street, 01382 739 277, Mon-Sat 9am-5pm; Sun 11am-4pm.

Something of a foodie all-rounder, Robertson has a butcher's, deli and licensed café on site, making it the only eatery in Dundee to be supplied by their own butcher. Much of the stock for all three comes from the local area, and almost everything is made in-house. They no longer open for dinner, but do, as might be expected, particularly good meaty breakfasts. **robertsonofbroughtyferry. co.uk**

Dr Noodles Fast and well-priced noodle dining, sit in or takeaway

Visocchi's Café Bustling café serving Italian favourites

The Ship Inn

■ 121 Fisher Street, Broughty Ferry, 01382 779176, Mon-Sun 11am–midnight.

Right on the waterfront, this free house's nautical theme includes a restaurant based on RRS Discovery's ward room. Between May and September, look out for dolphins from the wide picture windows. A recently installed cellar has put a focus on cask-conditioned ales, which join a wide range of draught beers and lagers. The small restaurant has a decent pub menu, and the bar serves snacks. **theshipinn-broughtyferry.co.uk**

The Speedwell Bar

■ 165-167 Perth Road, 01382 667783, Mon-Sat 11am-midnight; Sun 12.30pm-midnight.

Universally known as Mennie's

after a long-serving former landlady, this Edwardian West End institution is a fantastic example of a pub at once historical and bang up to date. Almost unchanged since it opened in 1903, down to the unbeatably welcoming atmosphere, it's always busy. The bar serves a great range of CAMRA-approved ales and over 100 single malts, but no food. **mennies.co.uk**

T Ann Cake

■ 27 Exchange Street, 01382 203950, Tue-Fri 10am-5pm; Sat 10am-4pm. Closed Sun/Mon.

Only in its second year, T Ann Cake has built a loyal following, enthusiastic about the enormous and varied home-made cakes, interesting daily specials like wasabi pea burgers or mackerel rarebit, laid-back atmosphere and personable owner Ann Rougvie. Everything is

Eat & Drink

handmade right down to home-cured pastrami, and it's particularly good for vegan and gluten-free foods.

t-ann-cake.blogspot.co.uk

The Tasting Rooms

■ 2 Whitehall Crescent, 01382 224188, Mon-Sat noon-3pm; 5-9.30pm. Closed Sun.

With a bistro and wine bar on the ground floor and mezzanine-level formal dining room and private dining facilities, The Tasting Rooms is certainly versatile. The food and drink menus also aim to please with over 100 wines by the glass, and a modern Anglo-French à la carte. Sourcing is local, with the owners even pulling in fish from their own boat.

thetastingrooms.com

The Trades Bar

■ 40 Nethergate, 01382 229494, Mon-Sat 10-midnight; Sun 11-midnight.

All tiled floors, stained glass windows and ornate cornicing, Tradeshouse is paradoxically cosy thanks to corner snugs, and friendly despite the enormous bouncer outside. Populated by Dundonians of every flavour, the Trades is loved by some for its traditional pub grub, by others for big screen sport and by all for its 30 draught beers, lagers, real ales and ciders.

belhavenpubs.co.uk

Visocchi's Café

■ 40 Gray Street, 01382 779 297, Tue 9.30am-5pm; Wed/Thu and Sun 9.30am-8pm; Fri/Sat 9.30am-10pm.

Constantly busy, particularly in summer when their excellent artisan ice cream gains legions of fans. Family-run and family friendly, they're open for everything from well-made coffee and cake to Italian evening meals of home-made pizza and pasta. It's assuredly casual dining, with a formula that has been successful since Marco Caira Sr. opened it in 1954.

Local Specialities

The east coast is famously fertile and rich with produce. The people here tended to preserve their food with smoke and the delicious Arbroath smokie is still made by hanging a pair of haddock over hot woodsmoke until they are cooked. British marmalade was invented in 18th century Dundee when a merchant bought up a quantity of Seville oranges from a Spanish ship; when his wife found they were too bitter to eat, she cooked them with sugar, and Keiller's jam was born. Dundee cake is a delicious feast of spices, dried fruit, lemon and almonds cooked into a traditional rich fruit cake. Just to the north in Forfar, the bridie is sold as an individual pie made from shortcrust pastry and chuck steak and onion, and is still a very popular snack today.

Nightlife

Dundee has always had an excellent reputation for live music. Today's nightlife has extended beyond the smoky venues and crowded pubs and includes casinos, superclubs and even Saturday night lectures. Whatever you're in the mood for, there's bound to be some nightlife for you.

DUNDEE
ONE CITY, MANY DISCOVERIES

Art Bar
■ 140b Perth Road, 01382 227888. Mon-Sun noon-late

Across the road from the Art School, this cosy basement bar has a mixed clientele of students and professionals. The menu features snacks and bar food, and there is a wide selection of reasonably priced drinks. Live music is a feature at the weekend, and the walls are frequently adorned with the work of local artists. The atmosphere is lively and unpretentious, with welcoming bar staff on hand. Well worth a visit.

Caird Hall
■ City Square, 01382 434451

Caird Hall stands in the heart of Dundee overlooking City Square, a grand building renowned for its ten impressive Doric columns. Inside, the building is contemporary yet traditional, with multi-functional facilities bringing the venue up to date. From opera and comedy to pop and rock, Caird Hall has famously played host to the Beatles, Elton John and David Bowie in the past. It remains an important part of Dundee's history and cultural scene.

BOWIE AND THE BEATLES PLAYED THE CAIRD HALL

cairdhall.co.uk

Chambers
■ 59-61 Gellatly Street. Open daily

Chambers is experiencing a new lease of life since starting to host gigs. The clientele has become younger, with the student population clocking on to the relaxed atmosphere and affordable drinks menu, which offers a selection of very reasonably priced beers and wine. On top of this, gigs are free. If you are interested in seeing a band, arrive a bit before the listed start time to ensure good seats, as it's a small venue.

myspace.com/ chambersbardundee

Cinemas
Dundee has a good selection of cinemas, showing everything from arthouse shorts to Hollywood blockbusters.

■ **Cineworld**, Camperdown Park, Kingsway West, 0871 200 2000, cineworld.co.uk

■ **DCA Cinema**, 152 Nethergate, 01382 909900, dca.org.uk

■ **Odeon Cinema**, Douglas Road, 01382 504367, odeon.co.uk

Nightlife

G Casino High-rollers head here for a great night out

Clarks on Lindsay Street

■ 80 North Lindsay Street, 01382 224925. Mon/Thur 11am-midnight; Fri 11am-2.30am; Sat 12noon-2.30am; Sun 12noon-midnight.

Dundee's latest late night pub is ideally situated within the nightlife part of town. Perfect for those who are less inclined for nightclubs but still like to socialise into the wee hours. A quirky contemporary interior with frequent live bands and artists, check their website for latest events. A good mix of people especially on the weekend creating a very comfortable atmosphere. **clarksonlindsaystreet.com**

Couture Cocktail Bar and Restaurant

■ 314 Brook Street, 01382 739782. Mon/Fri 5pm-midnight; Sat midday-midnight; Sun: 4pm-midnight.

Broughty Ferry's modern cocktail bar & restaurant. Just round the corner from the train station, Couture is the ideal get away from the city. With a beautiful interior and fully stocked bar offering quality draught beers to a fine range of wines and spirits. It feels like you could be sat in ritzy London bar. Perfectly centred amongst other nightlife venues within Broughty Ferry as well.

DCA

■ 152 Nethergate, 01382 909900. Mon-Sat 10am-midnight; Sun noon-midnight

The Jute Café is Dundee's home to the professional post-work drinking crowd. It reaches capacity on Friday nights between 6.30pm and 10pm so be sure to book a table or arrive early. There are plenty of cocktails and a large selection of exciting wines and beers, complemented by a lovely menu, in the restaurant and the bar area. The bar is adjacent to the DCA cinema and a large patio. **dca.org.uk**

Nightlife

We've got it covered.

What's on across the UK

The most comprehensive events listings, award-winning writing and reviews, eating & drinking guides and much more.

list.co.uk

BOOKS COMEDY DANCE KIDS MUSIC THEATRE ART CLUBS FI

The Doghouse

■ 15 Ward Street, 01382 206812

The Doghouse has recently moved and is now housed in a converted church. Despite its new location, the regulars have remained faithful, providing a buzzing atmosphere. This establishment prides itself on hosting less mainstream acts than the nearby Fat Sam's. The Facebook page is packed with information on all of the upcoming events, and seldom does a night go by without a performance. Open Mic Night comes highly recommended. **facebook.com/ dundeedoghouse**

Duke's Corner

■ 13 Brown Street, 01382 205052. Mon-Sun noon-midnight

An impressive building with a large beer garden, Duke's is situated in the old Doghouse building. In keeping with the previous tenants, Duke's is a live music venue and hosts an array of gigs and comedy nights. The interior has been smartened up with two areas – the main bar and the performance area. The Duke's Corner is a popular choice for a more unique night out with its laid-back, jazz club-style set-up and a wide selection of beers on offer. **dukescorner.co.uk**

Dundee Rep

■ Tay Square, 01382 223530

See Culture, page 35

DUSA

■ Airlie Place

DUSA has a long history of being an award winning Student Union playing host to big acts such as Groove Armada, Biffy Clyro and Radio 1 DJs. With five levels, four bars and an impressive games room there is a theme to please even the pickiest of clientele. The epic legacy of "Skint" cheapness on a Tuesday night has to be seen to be believed . . . you will not be disappointed! Just remember your student ID to get in and take advantage of the 'cheapest prices' 7 days a week. **dusa.co.uk**

DUSA HAS HOSTED BIG ACTS SUCH AS GROOVE ARMADA & BIFFY CLYRO

Fat Sam's

■ 31 South Ward Road, 01382 228181

One of Dundee's top gig and comedy venues, Fat Sam's mixes established and popular bands with newer, more edgy local-bred music. It is also the Dundee home of Just Laugh, who put on comedy nights around Central Scotland. The impressive listings are available on its website. There is a mixture of customers, depending on what is showing, and though not intimate, the atmosphere is relaxed and friendly. **fatsams.co.uk**

Grovenor Casino

■ 142 West Marketgait, 01382 309120. Open 24 hours.

Dundee's newest casino, G Casino is a slick operation; the

Nightlife

all-day licence means it can cater for revellers whatever the time of day. As well as the gaming areas, G offers a modern restaurant and elegant bar, often with entertainment. The well-designed interior and extensive drinks list makes this a venue for a trendy crowd, whether they're playing the tables or not. **gcasino.co.uk/dundee**

Gardyne Theatre

■ Gardyne Road, 01382 448876

The proscenium arch Gardyne Theatre is east of Dundee on the Dundee College campus. Local societies are heavily involved with the theatre regularly showcasing local talent as well as special guest performances. From musicals, stage shows and orchestral to comedy the 404 seater Gardyne Theatre is bound to offer something that takes your fancy. Keep an eye on their website for their latest events. **dundeecollege.ac.uk/gardynetheatre**

Laing's Bar & Kitchen

■ Roseangle, 01382 228 250. Mon/Sat 11.30am-midnight; Sun 11.00am-11.30pm

Situated close to the University of Dundee campus Laing's is very popular. In the sunny days of summer the south facing beer garden out back is the place to spend a lazy afternoon. Especially when the outside bar is open! And if you are feeling a bit peckish the kitchen offers up some superb food at reasonable prices from 11am-9pm, 7 days a week. With a fresh menu ranging from traditional pub fare to daily specials there is a taste to suit everyone. **laingsbar.co.uk/**

Liquid and Envy

■ 21 South Ward Road, 0845 313 2584. Wed, Fri & Sat 10.30pm-2.30am

Dundee's newest club offers a twin clubbing experience. One entry fee gains access to two different scenes. Giant screens surround the dance floor in Liquid as chart music is pumped

DCA's Jute Café A great selection of cocktails and laid back tunes

Public Lectures

The University of Dundee has a world-class reputation in many departments, and has found ways of reaching out to include Dundonians in academic discussion and the latest research. This policy is encapsulated in the tradition of the Saturday Evening Lecture Series which takes place between January and May. These lectures cover a huge range of subjects from geographical exploration to psychology; they are given by experts in their field, some of whom are household names. The university also hosts the Bell Lecture Series, with respected academic speakers from the field of education. Details about the

above series are available on the University of Dundee website. Another initiative by the university is the café science talks, where current science issues can be discussed over a cup of coffee.

- cafesciencedundee.co.uk
- dundee.ac.uk/ externalrelations

---

from the speakers. Envy has more themed music nights such as 80s, 90s or R'n'B. The crowd is young (and sometimes in fancy dress) and drinks are generally cheap.
liquidclubs.com/dundee

Nether Inn

- 134 Nethergate,
01382 349970. Mon/Fri midday-midnight; Sat/Sun 12:30pm-midnight.

Across the road from the Overgate, the lively Nether Inn offers a welcome relief from retail therapy, with a mix of clientele, although mostly made up of students from local universities. The weekly pub quiz is well known for its tough questions and great banter. The colourful mismatch décor is best

described as alternative. The friendly bar staff give fantastic customer service. **screampubs. co.uk/thenetherinndundee**

Out Nightclub

- 124 Seagate. Wed-Sun, 11pm-2.30am

The only gay nightclub in Dundee, Out is defined by all accounts as a really great night out. Fresh and fun, each night has a different theme, from Wicked Wednesday to Chill Out Sunday, with Freak Out Friday starting the weekend off with a bang. Music comes courtesy of the three DJs, who take requests and really know how to get the party started. Cheap entry and drinks promos each night mean it won't break the bank.

The Phoenix
■ 103 Nethergate, 01382 200014. Mon–Sun 11am–midnight

A small, shabby-looking pub on this busy street has been open for about 150 years. All the more endearing for its scuffed edges, locals and students congregate here together under the stained-glass window. With an excellent choice of ales and beers, the Phoenix gets very busy at weekends. It's likely to be around for another 100 years.

The Reading Rooms
■ Blackscroft, 01382 228496 (enquiries made through Groucho's)

The Reading Rooms has established itself as an alternative, chilled out club, hosting a sparkling array of DJs in its quirky building, an old schoolhouse. Drinks are moderately priced, with friendly bar and door staff. The atmosphere is more relaxed than many other clubs in Dundee, and the clientele are generally very friendly. It has recently hosted acts as diverse as Mr Scruff and Jazzy Jeff. Head here for the DJ nights and you won't be disappointed. **myspace.com/ thereadingrooms**

Social
■ 10 South Tay Street, 01382 202070. Mon /Sun 11:45-midnight.

In the heart of the Cultural Quarter of the city. Social is a modern, bright venue with a relaxed atmosphere. With a separated informal lounge and buzzing dance floor area to the rear there is a taste for most. Mainly students, aimed nights through the week offering bingo, pub quiz and karaoke. Open mic nights are always well received. Check out their Facebook for daily management specials. **facebook.com/SocialDundee**

Tally's Bar & Kitchen
■ 11 Old Hawkhill, 01382 224777. Mon/Sat 11:00am-midnight; Sun 12:30pm-midnight.

TONIC IS QUITE A SMALL BAR, LOVELY ON A WEEK NIGHT

Located right on the door step of Dundee University, Tally's is a very trendy upmarket style bar. Recently refurbished with regular live entertainment there is a formal whilst relaxed atmosphere. Well recognised for their great cocktails at affordable prices. Typically, Tally's is popular with professionals at the weekend or students through the week.

Tay Bridge Bar
■ 129 Perth Road, 01382 643973. Mon/Sat 11.30am-midnight; Sun 11.00am-11.30pm

One of Dundee's oldest traditional pubs, the Tay Bridge Bar nestles on the Perth Road and has recently undergone welcome refurbishment. A must-visit bar, with quality period features and atmosphere to

Underground Guest DJs, student nights and well-priced entry

match. Popular with students and professionals it's only a 10 minute walk into the busy city centre but far enough away if that isn't your scene.

Tonic
■ 141 Nethergate, 01382 226103

Located right in the middle of Dundee's student area, Tonic's main clientele are students of all ages. Its menu is affordable, offering deals on cocktails, coffee and beer. It prides itself on a huge burger menu, which is a novelty if you feel hunger pangs while out for a drink. It is quite a small bar, lovely on a week night when you can hear yourself think, more difficult at weekends when it fills to bursting.

Underground
■ 25 South Tay Street, 0845 166 6025

Hidden away on the edge of the university area, Underground frequently hosts student nights, as well as special DJ nights. The DJ nights can either feature their resident acts or, less frequently, special guests. Prices depend on which night it is, although generally they are very reasonable. Entry fee and clientele vary depending on the event.

The Westport Bar
■ 66 North Lindsay Street, 01382 200008

Located close to many of Dundee's nightclubs, for some people the Westie may just be a place to stop for a quick pint. However, the bar has its own charm and an excellent reputation for live music and new bands. Previous names to grace the stage in the live venue area include Paolo Nutini as well as local bands.

Whitehall Theatre
■ 112 Bellfield Street, 08717 029 486

See Culture, page 39

stay

Rest your weary head in some of Dundee's best places to stay. Whether it's global chains, luxury independents or refurbished hostels, Dundee offers a range of accommodation to suit everyone's tastes and pockets.

DUNDEE
ONE CITY, MANY DISCOVERIES

Apex Dundee City Quay and Spa
■ 1 West Victoria Dock Road, 01382 202404

The luxury choice for accommodation in Dundee, the Apex Hotel is located in Dundee's City Quay, close to all local amenities. The design was the result of an ambitious art project, hence the striking exterior. Inside, the hotel offers modern facilities in a relaxing atmosphere. Metro, the restaurant and bar, has an excellent reputation (page 70) and is frequently visited by locals as well as hotel guests. A glass wall provides an abundance of light to the dining area, offering a view of the calm waters of the City Quay. Prices can start as low as £64.
apexhotels.co.uk

Discovery Quay Premier Inn
■ Riverside Drive, 08701 977 079

This riverside hotel is only a hop and a skip away from Dundee's famous Discovery Point. Simple rooms and reasonable prices make a stay in this hotel pleasant and unpretentious and the staff are friendly – always a bonus. City centre restaurants and pubs are within a short walking distance and there are beautiful riverside views right on the hotel's doorstep. There are two other Premier Inns, one on the outskirts of the city, and one in Broughty Ferry. **premierinn.com**

Dundee Carlton Hotel
■ 2 Dalgleish Road, 01382 462056

With only nine bedrooms, the Carlton adds a personal touch to your stay. The hotel has excellent views over the river and the recently refurbished rooms are clean and spacious, offering family accommodation as well as double rooms. The staff are helpful and the breakfast is well reputed.
dundeecarlton.com

Hilton Dundee
■ Earl Grey Place, 01382 229271

A large hotel near to the city centre, the Hilton Dundee features all the services you associate with an international hotel group, such as a swimming pool, room service and decent rooms. The great location means the central entertainment zone is within easy walking distance. Additionally, the hotel restaurant offers some fabulous views of the river. A popular choice with many visitors, especially for those travelling on business, the Hilton Dundee offers the reliable service that has made its name across the world.
hilton.co.uk/dundee

Holiday Inn Express
■ 41 Dock Street, 01382 314330

The Holiday Inn Express is a popular choice for business travel, due to its central location. Friendly staff and a glass-walled bar and breakfast area makes a

Apex Dundee City Quay and Spa Luxury with a great view

visit to the hotel a fresh and inviting experience. Being an express hotel, bathroom facilities stretch to showers only (no baths), but the rooms are adequate, and the doubles also contain a sofa for a third person. There's no restaurant but a continental breakfast is complimentary. Prices typically start at £84 but can be less during quieter periods. **holidayinnexpressdundee. com**

Hoppo Hostel
■ 71 High Street, 01382 224646

The clichéd image of a dingy hostel could not be further from the truth at Hoppo. The magnificently restored building hosts a mixture of single, double and multi rooms – all with secure electronic key access. Excellently located right in the middle of the pedestrian precinct of the city centre, the Hoppo Hostel boasts several communal areas for meeting new friends

including a guest kitchen, dining room, common room – with satellite TV – and pool room. Bedrooms are clean, and some have ensuite facilities. Amenities include free linen, towel hire and internet access. The reception is open from 8am to midnight and there is no curfew for late owls. Hoppo is a suitable stay for individuals and groups alike and the staff are always on hand to help out. **hoppo.com/dundee**

Hotel Broughty Ferry
■ 16 West Queen Street, Broughty Ferry, 01382 480027

On the road into Broughty Ferry sits this little hotel. The rooms are of a high standard, clean, comfortable and well looked after. It is a short walk from the centre of Broughty Ferry and the beach on the banks of the Tay. The restaurant serves simple but tasty food and the included breakfast is very good. A

Chris Van der Kuyl
Bright Solid

'There are lots of opportunities in Dundee. The city's really changed over the past ten years and there are plenty of prospects for people coming here now. Dundee is on the edge of a transformation. Major transform-ations tend to start off with a single, strong icon - take the Sydney Opera house for example. The Victoria & Albert at Dundee could do that for Dundee.'

Stay

swimming pool, sauna and solarium provid relaxing break before heading to the bar. Th friendly staff will do their utmost to help yo
hotelbroughtyferry.co.uk

Invercarse
■ 371 Perth Road, 01382 669231

Located on the Perth Road, near Dundee's cultural heart, the Invercarse Hotel manages to escape the noisy bustle of the city centre while still being within walking distance of attractions and local amenities. Set back fro the road via a leafy driveway, this Best Wes hotel offers a homely visit with good facilit amid slightly dated décor. Perfect for a slow paced visit to the city. Prices for a double ro start at £89.
bw-invercarsehotel.co.uk

Landmark
■ Kingsway West, 01382 641122

The Landmark has undergone a massive refurbishment, transforming it into a luxury hotel in grounds away from the road. You can expect a good standard of service with the tastefully decorated hotel, with the usua features of a restaurant and bar, room servi and TV/Wi-Fi. There is also a well-equippe leisure centre and pool. The hotel is a short distance from the city centre, in a good position for travel from the A90 and great f those with their own transport.
thelandmarkdundee.co.uk

Malmaison
■ coming soon

The imposing grey Victorian building that o was the Tay Hotel is at last to be rescued an transformed into a boutique hotel, reflecting building's illustrious past.

A thirty five year lease has just been signe with the well regarded Malmaison Hotel gr and a sigh of relief has been breathed by all those concerned with the waterfront projec The hotel is due to be refurbished by May 2 and soon the bad impression it gives as visi arrive at the railway station close by, will b swept away by its restoration. This is such a

Piperdam Lodges Countryside retreat perfect for adventurers

landmark building, not pretty but substantial and essential to the new vision for Dundee's Waterfront.

The place has been empty since 1997, so this news is a welcome announcement. The luxury hotel chain has engaged a respected architectural practise from Glasgow, Curious Design to add a modern frontage of brick, brushed steel and large glass openings with a new entrance and canopy on Dock Street. Two mezzanine levels will be added to the building and the stonework, cornicing and cupola in the domed roof will be restored. This was made possible by Dundee City Council granting planning permission for the renovation of B listed buildings.

Once refurbished, Malmaison Dundee will have ninety one bedrooms with generous bathrooms, a brasserie, private dining room, whisky snug and wine cellar. Malmaison's house style is known for its good quality, chic and comfortable furnishings, whilst the management make a point of sourcing locally produced food and drink whenever possible.

Dundee has no other boutique hotels so this will be a great addition and it is expected that the new V&A building will bring a lot more tourists to the city. **malmaison.com**

Piperdam Lodges

■ Piperdam Golf & Leisure Resort, Fowlis, 01382 581374.

Set in peaceful countryside Piperdam Lodges are highly regarded for their luxury and quality with a four star rating. Large groups may be interested in hiring one of the many spacious self-catering lodges boasting Jacuzzis and snooker tables. All lodges have mod-cons. Activities available include quad biking, golf, spa, swimming and fishing. The onsite restaurant is fantastic ranging from rolls and snacks, to a full a la Carte menu. **piperdam.com**

Stay

Westport Luxury Serviced Apartments 5 star penthouse living

Queen's Hotel

▨ 160 Nethergate, 01382 322515

Built in 1878, the Queen's Hotel is a huge building situated at the top of the Perth Road, close to the DCA and other bars, restaurants and attractions. The hotel has a decent reputation and offers the usual facilities found in a Best Western hotel, including free Wi-Fi. As well as the hotel's own restaurant, the choice of places to dine in the area is abundant. You'll be in good company – Sir Winston Churchill used the hotel as a base for his successful 1908 election campaign.

queenshotel-dundee.com

Taychreggan Hotel

▨ 4 Ellieslea Road, West Ferry, 01382 778626

Dating back to 1876, Taychreggan was once a private house and the ten-bedroom hotel is still privately owned. Offering some excellent river views, the hotel is also renowned for its beautiful garden, which can be appreciated from the sun terrace. In addition to the restaurant, the award-winning bar stocks more than 400 single malt whiskies and a good wine list. The location is also great, within close proximity to both Dundee and Broughty Ferry.

taychreggan-hotel.co.uk

THE CONCIERGE IS AVAILABLE TO CATER FOR YOUR NEEDS

Travelodge

▨ 152-158 West Marketgait, 0871 984 6301

A budget option if you book early, Travelodge has deals that can begin as low as £19. This branch gets busy at weekends, in large part due to its location near to the big nightclubs. While it may not be the most attractive building in the city, this hotel

Stay

is in a great location, making it an excellent choice for an overnight excursion to Dundee. Rooms include a TV and offer a pay-for-use Wi-Fi service.
travelodge.co.uk

Westport Luxury Serviced Apartments
■ 138 West Marketgait, 01382 313633

The only 5 star rated serviced apartments in Dundee. Offering all the luxury of a hotel but with the comforts of home. The penthouse is absolutely stunning. Located in the heart of the city these apartments are perfect for visiting business people or for leisure. A concierge is available 24 hours catering for any guests needs. Also a member of the prestigious Connoisseur Scotland group.
westportservicedapartments. com

Woodlands Hotel
■ 13 Panmure Terrace, Broughty Ferry, 01382 480033

The Woodlands is a small, intimate hotel, situated out of Dundee, but very near to Broughty Ferry. It is relaxed, with a friendly bar and smart restaurant. Reception staff are very helpful, and the rooms are clean and comfortable. There is a small leisure club in the hotel, housing a pool, gym, steam room and sauna. Book early to take advantage of good deals.
bw-woodlandshotel.co.uk

Career Driven

Dundee is a great place to work – both for locals and those wishing to relocate. The East Coast mainline makes it a relatively easy commute from both Edinburgh to the south and Aberdeen to the north. Figures released in March 2012 show that Dundee is leading the way in keeping Scotland out of a double-dip recession with the biggest increase in permanent staff placements in the country.

Dundee's traditional industries have been slowly overtaken by a new and thriving economy, with biomedical and biotechnology research and development, and the computer games industry at the forefront.

There is a close link between academia and industry in Dundee, which can only help strengthen commerical enterprise in the city. Dundee University has spun out 20 companies in the past ten years, generating over £89m in annual turnover and creating over 300 jobs in the city – no mean feat for an academic institution. Meanwhile, world renowned games, computer arts and related degrees at The University of Abertay Dundee feed into the city's games development studios.

Jobs continue to be created with the redevelopment of the city, another key factor in the city's renewed energy. More and more people are attracted to the benefits of Dundee.
locate-dundee.co.uk

Explore

Ideally located in the heart of the country, Dundee is a great base for anyone looking to explore the best of what Scotland has to offer. From mountain climbing to sand yachting, Pictish trails or Peter Pan, there's a wealth of exciting things to do within a short distance of the city centre.

DUNDEE
ONE CITY, MANY DISCOVERIES

Arbroath Abbey A magnificent landmark in the coastal town

Angus Pictish Trail

■ The trail leaflet can be picked up at Pictavia Visitor Centre, Brechin, 01356 623050. Mon-Sat 9am-5pm; Sun 10am-5pm. Admission £3.25 adult. The stones are freely accessible in the landscape or preserved in small museums open between Apr-Sep. Check the website for access details. The trail can also be downloaded from **pictavia.org.uk**

The Picts lived in what is now north east Scotland around 2000 years ago. The impressive carved stones that can be seen on this trail were probably memorial stones, carved with heraldic symbols, beasts and scenes from important events such as the Battle of Dunnichen in 685. After conversion to Christianity the Pictish stonemasons added elaborate crosses to their repertoire. The trail takes up to four days; a visit to Pictavia, an interpretive centre, gives the context. Highlights include the sculptured stones at Aberlemno, in the Meffan Institute, St Vigean's and Meigle Museums.

Arbroath Abbey

■ Abbey Street, Arbroath, 01241 878756. Apr-Sep: Mon-Sun 9.30am-5.30pm; Oct-Mar: 9.30am-4.30pm. Admission £4.70

The sandstone ruins are a magnificent landmark in this coastal town. The abbey was founded in 1178 by William the Lion and built as a memorial to Thomas Becket. It is famous for the 1320 Declaration of Arbroath when the earls and barons of Scotland wrote to the pope affirming their independence from England and their allegiance to Robert the Bruce. The abbey ruins are impressive, especially the church façade and Abbot's House, and the visitor centre is packed with historical displays.
historic-scotland.gov.uk

Brechin Castle Centre

■ Haughmuir, Brechin, 01356 626813. Mon-Fri 9am-5pm (6pm summer only), Sat 9am-6pm, Sun 10am-6pm. Admission to country park £3.50

This large retail centre selling plants, food and gifts, linen and books, also has an exciting play area in a country park with an ornamental lake, nature trails, model farm and a restaurant serving home baking. The landscaping has still to mature but there is something to suit the whole family here. The centre is beside Pictavia, a visitor attraction that tells the story of the Picts.

brechincastlecentre.co.uk

Caledonian Steam Railway

■ The Station, Park Road, Brechin. 01356 622992. Jun & Sep: Sun; Jul & Aug: Sat & Sun. Admission varies

A group of volunteers run summer weekend train rides from here for four miles into the Angus countryside to the Bridge of Dun station. Within walking distance is the House of Dun, an 18th century house and gardens open to the public. Special offers run throughout the year.

caledonianrailway.co.uk

Eden Estuary Nature Reserve

■ 01333 429785

A short drive over the Tay Road Bridge and you will come across this rich intertidal landscape. Home to millions of plants and animals with a healthy population of birds. Including four species of Geese that can regularly be seen here in Autumn and Winter. The Eden Estuary centre is just after the town of Guardbridge. Parking may be charged depending on the car park you choose.

fifecoastandcountry- sidetrust.co.uk

Glamis Castle

■ 01307 840393, 15 Mar-Oct: 10am-6pm, Nov-31 Dec: 10.30am-4.30pm. Closed Dec 24-26. Admission £6 (adult)

This is one of Scotland's must-see destinations. Just to go down the straight oak-lined avenue with the castle at the end is a spectacular experience. The supposedly haunted building, where HM Queen Elizabeth, the Queen Mother, grew up, is steeped in history and filled with wonderful furniture, tapestry, china and pictures. You can get freshly cooked food in the Victorian kitchen restaurant and pick up souvenirs in the gift shop outside. Leave time to walk around the Italian garden and parklands planted with superb mature trees. The 17th century monumental sundial in the grounds is worth a special detour and, if you have children with you, they'll want a shot on the playground and a look at the highland cattle. At the village end of one of the avenues,

ARBROATH ABBEY WAS BUILT AS A MEMORIAL TO THOMAS BECKET

Explore

close to the village church, is the ancient St Fergus's Well. If you walk there, take a look at the Pictish stone and then peek into the cottage museum about Angus folklore. The castle and grounds host a variety of events, including a classical music prom, highland games and a countryside festival. **glamis-castle.co.uk**

Glendoick Garden Centre and Restaurant
■ A90 Perth-Dundee Road, 01738 860260, Mon-Sat 9am-5pm, Sun 10am-5pm (slightly longer hours in the summer). Closed 25 & 26 Dec, 31 Dec-4 Jan

This garden centre is owned by the Cox family, Dundee jute manufacturers who turned plantsmen, famous for their plant-hunting expeditions over three generations. Check out the website for their private garden openings. The family sell specialist azaleas and rhododendrons, many bred by them. The centre also sells food and everything for the garden, with the emphasis on hardy plants suitable for the Scottish climate. There is a café and an attractive display garden where you can see the plants growing before you buy. **glendoick.com**

Glenshee
■ Cairnwell Pass, 013397 41320

The glen of fairies is a beautiful place in all seasons. Known for its walking in the summer and for great skiing in the winter, it is about one hour's drive from Dundee. When the snow is good and the wind factor is not too strong you can imagine yourself in the Alps. Facilities are basic, but ski hire is easily arranged, as are lessons in snowsports. There is 40 km of marked piste, with plenty of scope for the intermediate skier/snowboarder on the twenty-six blue and red runs and two exciting black runs for the skilful. Beginners are also well looked after with nursery slopes and green runs. The surrounding hills are wonderful to walk in at all times of the year, with a Corbett (2500ft high) mountain, Ben Gulabin, approached from Spittal of Glenshee. **ski-glenshee.co.uk**

Golf Practise your putt at some of Scotland's most beautiful courses

Golf

The golf courses of Dundee have always had to live in the shadow of their more famous neighbouring courses, but within the city environs are six courses that merit the attention of any golfer. The council owns and runs Caird Park and Camperdown, both offering very affordable golf to all. Camperdown especially is one of the better undiscovered parkland courses of Scotland and deserves much wider recognition. Downfield is an Open Championship qualifying course and one of the best inland courses you will find. Ballumbie Castle and Piperdam are both relatively new parkland-type courses based around housing developments and they both offer a good test for golfers of all abilities. Monifieth is the nearest of the famed stretch of Angus links courses to Dundee and offers two 18-hole courses. The Medal course is another Open Championship qualifying course and Carnoustie plays regular host to The Open.
eastofscotlandgolf.com

■ **Ballumbie Castle**, Old Quarry Road, Off Ballumbie Road, 01382 730026, ballumbiecastle golfclub.com/
■ **Caird Park**, Mains Loan, 01382 438871, dundeecity.gov .uk/golf/main.htm
■ **Camperdown Country Park**, Coupar Angus Road, 01382 431820, dundeecity.gov.uk/ golf/ main.htm
■ **Carnoustie Country** carnoustiecountry.com
■ **Downfield**, Turnberry Avenue, 01382 825595, downfieldgolf.co.uk/
■ **Monifieth Golf Links**, Monifieth Links, Princes Street, Monifieth, 01382 532767, monifiethgolf.co.uk
■ **Piperdam Golf & Leisure Resort**, Fowlis, 01382 581374, piperdam.com/

JM Barrie's Birthplace
■ 9 Brechin Road, Kirriemuir, 01575 572646/0844 4392142. Opening times vary, call for details. Admission £5.50

Barrie, creator of Peter Pan and one of ten children, was born in this charming 19th-century two-storey cottage in 1860. That the family lived modestly is reflected in the furnishings. No 11 is fitted out as an exhibition space where you can see manuscripts and theatrical costumes worn in the stage productions of *Peter Pan*. Outside, willow is fashioned into a crocodile. Pirate workshops take place, with children enjoying crafts and games.

Land Yachting
■ West Sands, St Andrews, 07784 121125

Land yachting, a relatively new sport, is available on beaches near to Arbroath and St Andrews. The year-round activities offered by local business Blown Away include special family days, childrens' sports and even stag and hen parties. It also offers kayaking, and occasionally 'beach Olympics' competitions. An action-packed day out with family or friends.
blownawaylandyachts.co.uk

Explore

Lunan Bay
■ Inverkeilor

The beach of choice for many Dundonians is about 40 minutes in the car. This is a place to walk for hours, or surf, or swim. The sand is pale and fine though studded in parts with gloriously coloured pebbles. When the tide is very high, it is possible to walk along the top of the sand dunes. The southern end of the beach leads to a coastal path which meanders for about seven miles, ending in Auchmithie and taking you excitingly close to the sandstone cliffs. In the nesting season, you can see puffins on the cliff edges and, looking inland, see the hills of Angus rising beyond the cultivated fields.

Montrose Basin Local Nature Reserve
■ 01674 676336. Visitor Centre; 1 Mar to 31 Oct: open daily from 10.30am-5pm; 1 Nov to 28 Feb: open Fri to Sun from 10.30am-4pm. Closed on 25 & 26 Dec and 1 & 2 Jan.

Traveling about 45 mins east of Dundee and you'll come to the fine town of Montrose. The reserve allows for leisure activities including walking, bird watching, sailing, fishing, wildfowling and bait digging. If you want to explore by yourself wildfowl are present all year round. The Scottish Wildlife Trust have a visitor centre, for which there is a small fee, and a programme of events on their website, Overwintering geese and April to August for sandmartin are two highlights.

Perth Racecourse
■ Scone Palace Park, Perth, 01738 551597 (ticket hotline). Season runs from Apr-Sep

If you've never had a trip to the races, then Perth Racecourse

Cycling

The Green Circular is an illuminating route that encompasses the whole of the city and its outskirts. Designed as a way to see parts of the city you wouldn't discover otherwise, it has been devised to include as few roads as possible, so is very family friendly and safe for all ages and for the less experienced cyclist. The east section leaves central Dundee via the old docks and heads towards Broughty Ferry, with beautiful Tay views along the way. It passes through a quaint

nature reserve and into Monifieth. It doubles back around the green northern areas of the city before passing around Ninewells Hospital and heading back into the centre. If you want to tackle only a part of it, go for the Dundee to Broughty Ferry path: the views are unrivalled.

Explore

Perth Racecourse Try to back a winner at Perth Races

is the perfect place to start. This award-winning course is considered to be a good testing ground for the bigger races later in the season. City of Perth Gold Cup Day, held in late May, is one of the biggest events here, usually attracting over 11,000 spectators.
perth-races.co.uk

Scone Palace
■ Perth, 01738 552300.
Apr-Oct: Mon-Fri & Sun
9.30am-5pm; Sat 9.30am-4pm.
Closed Nov-Mar. Admission £9
(Adult)

Once the place where the Kings of Scotland were crowned, and rightful home to the Stone of Destiny (now in Edinburgh Castle), Scone Palace is a vital key in understanding the history of the country. Situated just outside Perth, Scone Palace is still a family home (to the Earls of Mansfield), and an extremely popular visitor attraction. As well as touring the Palace and the splendid

grounds, there are often events taking place here, from the Scottish Game Fair to the International Horse Trials.
scone-palace.co.uk

Sidlaw Hills
■ Sidlaw Hills

This band of hills to the north of Dundee provides a stunning view over Tayside. Walkers of all abilities should be able to enjoy this walk in the spring-autumn seasons. However in the winter less experienced walkers should take caution. Waterproofs and warm clothing is recommended as a precaution to changeable weather conditions. Parking is at an informal layby just north west of Knapp.

St Andrews
■ Fife

Old and new blends together in this ancient university town where the buildings date from as early as the 13th century.

Explore

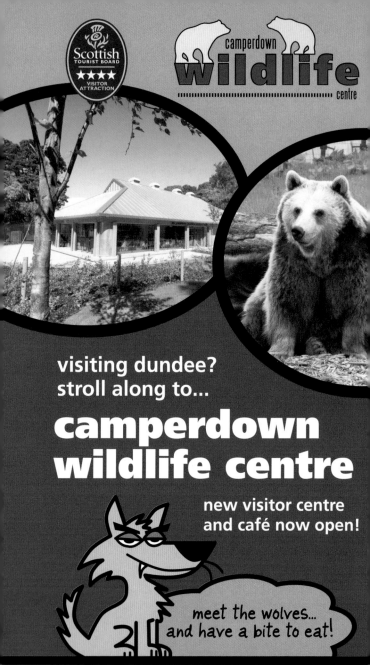

Legend says the relics of St Andrew were brought here by St Rule, some time before golf was invented here in the 15th century. The beach and the golf courses make it a great place for a holiday, while the closes and streets are fun to explore.

Tentsmuir Nature Reserve and Beach

■ 01382 553704

Across the Tay Bridge, a mile and a half from Tayport, this nature reserve has a stunning beach, forest walks, wild-fowling hides by three freshwater lochs and a species-rich dune heath. You can walk from Tayport or approach it from the Forestry Commission car park off the B945. The butterflies, flowers, birds and seals are in their element here. **tentsmuir.org**

Wind surfing

■ Monikie Country Park, 01382 370202. May-Sep

In the beautiful Monikie Country Park, Adventure Scotland provides both windsurfing taster sessions and more serious training. The sessions run in the summer months with tasters usually held in the evenings. The instructors are fully trained and offer encouragement to beginners of all ages. The park also offers kayaking, trout fishing, a locally famous adventure playground and Byzantium (page 67) run a café here. **adventure. visitscotland.com**

The Angus Glens

From Dundee it is 17 miles to Kirriemuir where the landscape changes to wild moorland and hills. There are six main glens: Prosen, Ogil, Lethnott, Isla, Clova and Esk. They all include rivers or burns with grassland, livestock and birch trees alongside, rising to heather. There is very good walking in all the glens with a number of Munros (mountains over 3000ft) easily reached and several marked paths, such as Jock's Road from Glen Clova to Braemar. A walking festival is held every June, with walks led by rangers. **angusahead.com/ walkingfestival**

Information

Dundee is in a great location for visitors from all over Scotland, the UK and the rest of the world. Easy to get to from Edinburgh, Glasgow and Aberdeen, this section will tell you how to get there and how to get around, and provide you with all the information you'll need for a great trip.

DUNDEE
ONE CITY, MANY DISCOVERIES

Travel & useful contact

Air
■ Dundee Airport (DDE),
Riverside, 01382 662200

Dundee is well-served by a
small but very convenient airport, located just beside the Tay.
Scheduled flights leave from
here for London City, Belfast
City, Birmingham and Jersey in
the summer, and some chartered
package holidays depart from
here too – contact airlines and
tour operators for timetable
information (see website for details). The terminal has a small
café, and both long and short
stay car parks. The rail and bus
stations are only a five-minute
drive from the airport, taking the
stress out of connecting jour-
neys. While there are always
taxis waiting, a bus service into
the city centre operates too.
hial.co.uk/dundee-airport.html

Car Hire
■ **Arnold Clark**, East Dock
Street, 01382 225382,
arnoldclarkrental.com
■ **Europcar**, 45-53 Gellatly
Street, 01382 455505,
europcar.co.uk
■ **Thrifty Car & Van Rental**,
Kingsway Park, 01382 621169,
thrifty.co.uk

Coach & Bus
■ Dundee Bus Station, Seagate,
0871 200 2233 (Travel Line)
01382 614550 (other enquiries)

Dundee is well-served by
cross-country coaches, and
National Express, Megabus and
Stagecoach operate services to
and through the city. National
Express also operates within the
city itself, offering Day Saver
tickets, which are handy for
covering a lot of ground in one
day. See individual company
websites for more details.

nxbus.co.uk/dundee,
uk.megabus.com,
stagecoachbus.com

Cycle Hire
■ **Spokes**, 272 Perth Road,
01382 666644,
spokescycles.net

General information
For more information on, and to
sign up for regular newsletters
about Dundee, One City, Many
Discoveries, see the website.
dundee.com

Newspapers
■ **The Courier**
Mon-Sat, thecourier.co.uk
■ **Evening Telegraph**
Mon-Fri, eveningtelegraph.co.uk

NHS 24
■ 08454 242424, nhs24.com
■ NHS 24 Tayside Local Centre Wallacetown Health Centre, Lyon Street.

Ninewells Hospital
■ Ninewells Avenue, 01382 660111, nhstayside.scot.nhs.uk

Pedal & Foot
One of the best things about a compact city centre is the ability to get around under your own steam. The Dundee Travel Info website has information on cycling routes as well as a handy walk planner.
dundeetravelactive.com

Road
Dundee is well-connected to the rest of the UK, being on the A90 from Glasgow and Edinburgh to Aberdeen. There is also a scenic route from Edinburgh through Fife and into Dundee over the Tay Road Bridge.

Tayside Police
■ West Bell Street, 0300 111 2222 (non-emergency number), 01382 591591 (lost & found property). Call 999 or 112 in an emergency. tayside.police.uk

Taxis
■ **Dundee 50 50 50**, 01382 505050
■ **Dundee Private Hire**, 01382 203020, dundeecabs.com
■ **Skycabs Direct**, 01382 500555, dundeetaxis.com
■ **Tay Taxis**, 01382 450450, tay-taxis.co.uk
■ **Tele-Taxis** 01382 825 825, tele-taxis.co.uk

Train
■ Dundee Railway Station (DEE), South Union Street, 08457 48 49 50 (National Rail Enquiries)

Again, the city benefits from excellent rail links as it is on both the Edinburgh and Glasgow mainline to Aberdeen. The station is within walking distance of most of the city centre. Check the Trainline and National Rail websites for timetables.
nationalrail.co.uk, thetrainline.com

Visitor Information
■ VisitScotland Information Centre, Discovery Point, 01382 527527

Dundee's main tourist infomation centre is handily located at Discovery Point, and staff there will be happy to help with all aspects of your stay.
angusanddundee.co.uk, dundee.com

City centre map

Dudhope Terrace

Constitution Road

Dudhope Stre

Barrack Road

Opal 1

Dudhope Park

A923 LOCHEE ROAD

A991 NORTH MARKETGAIT

Abert
Uni

Ash Street

P

Abertay
Library

Police
HQ

Douglas Street

West Henderson's Wynd

Blinshall Street

A991 WEST MARKETGAIT

Court

West Bell Street

Miln Street

Ward Road

Verdant
Works

North Lindsay Street

South Ward Road

P

Brook Street

Guthrie Street

Travelodge
Westport
Apartments

Willi

P

Hawkhill

West Port

P

A991 WEST MAR

Hawkhill

Institute of
Sport and
exercise

Dalhousie

Park Place

South Tay Street

Dundee
Rep

Old Hawkhill

Queen
Mother
Building

Wellcome
Trust Biocentre

Belmont
Residences

Small's Wynd

Bonar
Hall

Nethergate

De

University
of Dundee

University
of Dundee

Sensation
Dundee

Springfield

DJCAD
College of Art
& Design

Airlie Place

Queen's
Hotel

Greenma

Perth Road

Magdalen Green

To Perth, Edinburgh & Glasgow A90

dee Airport

Information

Due to the £1 billion regeneration of Dundee's Waterfront the road fabric of the city is changing to accommodate the new layout. For this reason there will be changes not reflected on this map over the coming months. For up to date information visit **dundeewaterfront.com**

Information

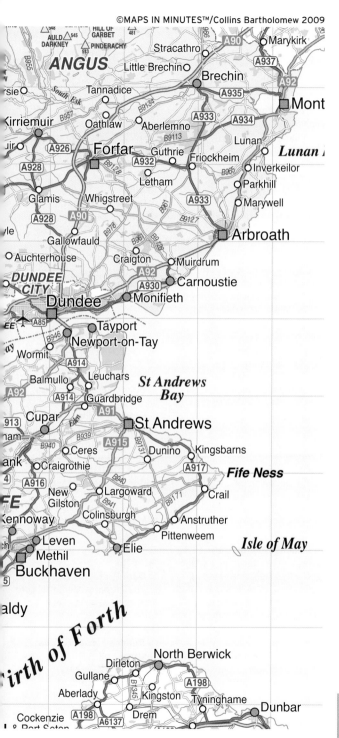

Events Calendar

Year-round
■ **Dundee Farmers' Market**
High Street, 3rd Saturday of each month.

January
■ **New Year's Day Dook**
Broughty Ferry Harbour,
yeaaba.org.uk Start the year by braving the icy waters of the Tay.

March
■ **Dundee Women's Festival**
Various venues in the city, 01382 305731, **d-v-a.org.uk** A series of events about women's rights.

April
■ **Italian Film Festival**
Dundee Contemporary Arts, 01382 909900,
italianfilmfestival.org.uk
Annual celebration of the best of Italian cinema.

May
■ **Ignite**
Various venues
ignitedundee.co.uk
Ten-day celebration of creativity and culture across Dundee, Angus and Fife.

■ **Dundee Degree Show**
Duncan of Jordanstone College of Art & Design, University of Dundee, 01382 388828, **dundee. ac.uk/djcad/degreeshow**
Exhibition of the work of emerging artists.

■ **Craft Festival Scotland**
Venues throughout Scotland, 01382 383000, **dundee.ac.uk/ djcad**
Celebrating the diversity of craft in Scotland.

■ **Angus Glens Walking Festival**
Venues throughout Angus, 01575 550233, **angusahead. com/walkingfestival**
Walks for all in the Angus glens.

June
■ **Dundee WestFest**
Various venues in the West End, 07815 209905,
dundeewestfest.co.uk
Festival of Dundee talent.

■ **Seashore Festival**
Castle Green, Broughty Ferry, 01382 431848, **dundeecity. gov.uk**
Launching the summer season celebrating the seashore.

July
■ **Dundee Blues Bonanza**
Various venues in the city,
dundeebluesbonanza.co.uk
The 'Blues Capital of Scotland' hosts a free music festival.

■ **T in the Park**
Balado, Kinross, **tinthepark. com**
Enormous and beloved music festival, within easy reach of Dundee.

August
■ **Dare Protoplay**
Caird Hall, **daretobedigital.com**
Free video gaming event.

September
■ **Dundee Flower & Food Festival**
Camperdown Country Park, 01382 433815,
dundeeflowerandfoodfestival. com
Festival of food and drink.

■ Doors Open Days
Venues throughout Scotland, 0141 221 1466, **doorsopendays. org.uk**
Access to buildings that are usually kept under wraps.

■ RAF Leuchars Air Show
RAF Leuchars, 01334 839000, **airshow.co.uk**
Largest non-sporting outdoor event in Scotland.

October

■ Discovery Film Festival
Dundee Contemporary Arts, 01382 909900, **discoveryfilmfestival.org.uk**

International film festival for children and young people.

■ Dundee Literary Festival
Various venues in the city, 01382 384413, **literarydundee. co.uk**
Events with local and international authors.

■ Dundee Science Festival
Various venues in the city, 01382 868609, **dundeesciencefestival. org**
Family-friendly science festival.

November
■ Dundee Jazz Festival
Gardyne Theatre, 0845 111 0302, **jazzdundee.co.uk**
Jazz from international artists and local stars.

■ Dundee Mountain Film Festival
Bonar Hall, 01382 730699, **dundeemountainfilm.org.uk**
The UK's longest running mountain film festival.

■ NEoN
Various venues in the city, 01382 322852, **northeastofnorth.com**
Digital arts festival.

■ Christmas Light Night
City centre, 01382 434428, **dundee.com**
Dundee's major Christmas celebration, where the entire city centre is transformed into a performance area beginning with a magical torchlight procession and ending with two hours of partying and fireworks.

December
■ RSNO Christmas Concert
Caird Hall, 01382 434940, **rsno. org.uk**
Family-friendly concert.

Information

Index

Index

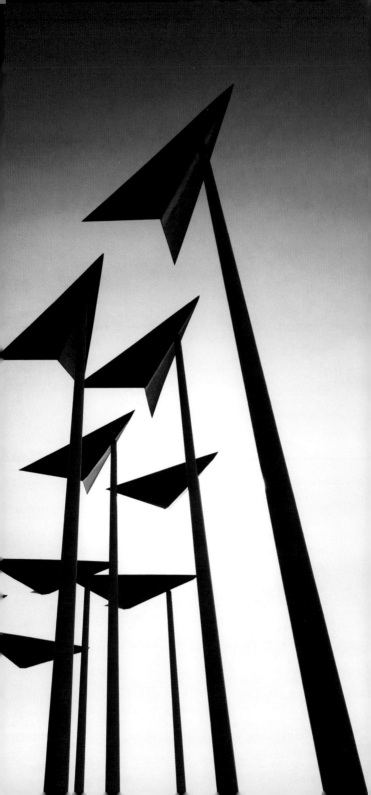

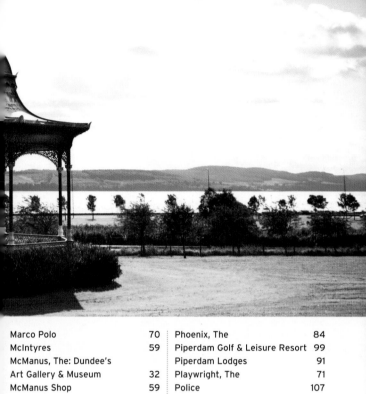

Index